3

TR

Turkish Cookery

Sally Mustoe

Turkish Cookery

SAQI

London   San Francisco

British Library Cataloguing-in-Publication Data
A catalogue record for this book is available from the British Library

ISBN 10: 0-86356-072-5
ISBN 13: 978-0-86356-072-9

Text copyright © retained by all contributors

This edition published 2006 by Saqi Books

A full cip record for this book is available from the British Library
A full cip record for this book is available from the Library of Congress

Design: Ourida Mneimne
Printed in Lebanon by Chemaly & Chemaly
Binding: Fouad El-Baayno Bookbinders

SAQI
26 Westbourne Grove, London W2 5RH
825 Page Street, Suite 203, Berkeley, California 94710
www.saqibooks.com

Contents

Acknowledgments

Most sincere thanks are due to the following for their valuable encouragement and practical help to the editor, Sally Mustoe, who is an enthusiastic consumer and not a cook: the Afiyet Olsun committee of Gönül Çilasun, Monica Hubner, Canan Maxton, Betty McKernan, Belma Ötüş-Baskett and the late Raphaela (Raff) Lewis (her humour and wit are greatly missed).

Thanks are also due to Andrew Clarke and Stephen Hubner (for legal advice), Naim Kula, Charlotte Mustoe and Dan Scarborough (for IT guidance), Hüseyin Özer, Philippa Scott, Osman Serim and the Turkish Gourmets Association in Istanbul, and to Mitch Albert of Saqi Books.

We are very grateful to the contributors – writers, chefs and photographers – who have donated their material.

Special thanks to Incilay Egeli, for her wonderful English translations of recipes by Turkish authors Sevim Gokyıldız, Ali Pasiner, Osman Serim, Nevin Halıcı, Vefa Zat and Turgul Şavkay.

Profits from the sale of this book will support the continuing education of Turkish children orphaned in Turkey's recurring earthquakes.

Preface

Sally Mustoe

The magnificent *Turks* exhibition at the Royal Academy of Arts in the spring of 2005 astonished both the general public and the experts, many of whom reluctantly admitted that there were great gaps in their knowledge of Turkey's cultural history.

Turkish food now needs similar treatment. The increase in tourism is partly responsible for more people becoming interested in Turkish cuisine. My own interest began forty years ago when two friends, Gwynneth and Sue, and I were on our way to Beirut, driving through Western Europe and some of the Arab states, then more perilously home through Eastern Europe. I was a BBC news and current affairs journalist and my first husband was a diplomat so I knew much of Europe and parts of the Middle East, but I hadn't previously visited Turkey. From our first few hours after landing at Izmir, I was in love with the scenery, the people and the food. Workmen in a lorry found humour in our situation when they stopped to mend our puncture. Then we came across a small boy dwarfed by a huge mound of melons. The knife he used to cut slices for us was nearly as big as his small frame, and he laughed as he watched us leaning over a ditch, biting into the moist flesh with the juice running down our chins. Later, when we stopped to admire the dramatic panoramic peaks of the Toros Mountains, we drank the first of many thousands of glasses of deliciously refreshing Turkish tea. Hugely popular and available throughout Turkey now, tea was only introduced generally to the country in the 1920s.

From numerous visits to Istanbul, I particularly cherish memories of eating fish by the Bosphorus at different restaurants around Bebek, near the home of my friends Charles Adelsen and Henry Angelo-Castrillon, who did so much for Turkish tourism in the 1970s and 80s. (*Midye tava* is still a favourite of mine, even though it is unfashionable now.) Further along that coast, past Sariyer, it is worth the lengthy bus journey out to Güzel Yer for the freshest sea *meze*, fish and fruit, overlooking the boats of all sizes coming from the Black Sea or crossing the Bosphorus.

Markets are always fascinating. In Muğla, the variety of fresh vegetables and fruit was impressive. Afterwards, my friends drove out of the town to a restaurant where we were given a large steaming platter of special rice piled high with the best goat meat I've ever had. Not far away, I thought I'd found the world's best honey, produced by bees in the pine-woods overlooking the lake at Köyceğiz, but I had to relegate it to second best when I tasted the chestnut honey in Gökçedere, a small village near Yalova.

I enjoyed the trout-only restaurant which jutted out over a river near Göçek, and the mushrooms bubbling in a cheese sauce cooked with the farm trout near Orhangazi. It is easy to appreciate why the members of the Turkish Gourmets Association, who made me welcome, value so highly the look, taste and smell of Turkish food.

Introduction

Raphaela Lewis

A publisher once said to me, paraphrasing Ecclesiastes, 'Of the writing of cookery books there is no end.' But this is no ordinary cookbook: it draws on one of the four seminal cuisines of the world – the others being Chinese, Italian and French – while retaining an elegant simplicity of taste and style.

The literal translation of *afiyet olsun* is 'let there be health'. Turks use this phrase where the French would say *bon appétit*, but it is also used after a meal to mean 'may it do you good'.

The Ottoman capital, Istanbul, inherited from Byzantium a cuisine of high quality and considerable amplitude. Its location blessed it with varieties of fish in the Bosphorus and the Golden Horn; the many market gardens and orchards provided vegetables and fruit; the farmlands, pastures and forests around contributed wheat, meat and game.

The city was also the terminus of many caravan routes and sea lanes. New flavours and skills were acknowledged and welcomed. Byzantine Greeks and returned refugees who had fled from Constantinople, Armenian and Jewish residents and immigrants, exchanges of population that brought Christian merchants and artisans from Asia Minor, the Aegean, the Balkans, and the north and south coasts of the Black Sea all contributed unfamiliar raw materials, styles and techniques which were readily accepted. Provincial governors, as well as merchants and travellers by land and sea, sent or brought back to the capital whatever food was new or interesting and the cuisine was thus further enriched. The first unfamiliar vegetables from the New World – green beans, peppers, tomatoes, gourds and so on – made their way to Istanbul from Europe via Genoa. Aubergines arrived from Moghul India and were at

once adopted and cultivated. By 1542 maize from America had already been domesticated and produced in Turkey. It became known in eastern and northern Europe as 'Turkish corn'.

The heart, and pride, of the Ottoman Empire was its capital, Istanbul, a city of immense beauty, privilege and authority. The focus of life in Istanbul was the Palace of the Sultans, the Saray. It covered an area of some ten acres, surrounded by a high wall 1,400 metres long. In the heart of the innermost precinct lay the *harem*, ruled over by the sultan's mother and home to the sultan's female relatives and other ladies of the court; beyond it were the Janissary Court, the Divan, the Mint, mosques, schools, hospitals, libraries, barracks and baths, pools and fountains, hunting enclosures and sports grounds, fuel stores and kitchens, snow-pits and ice-pits, armouries and stables – in fact, all that was necessary to maintain the pomp of the monarch. Small wonder that the palace employed 1,000 cooks and scullions cooking for between 5,000 and 10,000 people a day; hungry people who consumed in one year 30,000 chickens and 22,500 sheep, as well as jams, pickles, sweetmeats and sherbets in quantities which contemporary records described as simply beyond measure.

To illustrate the implications of providing for such a household, let me give you an example. South of Istanbul, across the Sea of Marmara, is the city of Bursa, capital of the Ottoman Empire until the conquest of Constantinople. It lies in the shadow of Uludağ, the Great Mountain, which is snow-capped for half the year. That snow was farmed by the sultan. At the top of the mountain it was shovelled and impacted firmly into blocks, wrapped completely in thick felt and transported on the backs of a train of mules, which descended the mountain in single file to Buzburnu, Ice Point, near the port of Mudanya. From there it was shipped across the Marmara in a vessel traditionally rowed by prisoners of war and brought, again by mule, into the city, where it was consigned to the palace. In the grounds of the palace, in the charge of the snow-keepers, the snow-pit was thus stocked and replenished. Any superfluous snow was distributed among the nine snow-pits in the city and offered for sale to the public. The keepers were answerable to the chief steward and from him to the chief cook, who ordered what he needed.

Sherbet – *şurup* – was the elegant drink, a concentrate of delicious flavours made of fruits, flowers and aromatics from all over the empire – *attar* of roses from Bulgaria, essence of ambergris from Yemen (there are seventy-eight recipes in one collection alone) – and stored away in bottles and earthenware jars. At the end of a banquet a silver goblet was filled with snow, and over the fragile crystalline mound was poured the concentrated essence of the delicate sherbet. *Afiyet olsun!*

The sophistication of Ottoman cuisine was, however, seldom reflected in the diet of ordinary people. The food eaten by the Turks consisted of what was easily acquired, such as game or wild plants; what was cultivated widely, like onions, garlic and root vegetables; what was grown locally according to soil and conditions, for example wheat on the central Anatolian plateau, or rice in the marshes; and what was commonly eaten everywhere, such as yoghurt. Occasionally, luxuries from more urban society were reserved for festivities such as weddings and circumcisions.

The basis (what dieticians refer to as 'filler') of the Turkish diet was most usually bulgur and honey or *pekmez*, a kind of molasses made of concentrated grape juice. The staples throughout Turkey were bread and yoghurt. Bread could be made with or without fat or sweeteners, kneaded with hands on the table or with paddles in a wooden bowl, shaped thick or thin, baked on a metal sheet over a fire in a small beehive-shaped outdoor oven or in a *tandır*, a sunken clay oven in the kitchen, or even in a communal *tandır* shared by perhaps twenty families and fuelled with chopped straw. It could be leavened or unleavened according to the region, and even to the time of year, since in harvest months when everyone was busy a flat pide was a quickly-made loaf that would keep well.

Yoghurt was brought by early Turcoman nomads from Central Asia and is perhaps Turkey's greatest contribution to the world. The word itself occurs in Turkish Buddhist texts from the eighth century onwards. It was made preferably with the milk of buffalo, but also of cow, goat or sheep, and was used for eating on its own and for cooking, diluted to make the drink *ayran*, drained to make cheese, and dried into dough-like cakes, in which form it could be preserved for months.

What both the sophisticated cuisine of the city and the food of ordinary people had in common was a certain simplicity in preparation and presentation. Taste was more important than appearance. Thus there was little difference between a dish prepared at the palace and one prepared at home, or in a restaurant, or bought from a professional retailer like a *muhallebici*. Of course, the kitchens in which the dishes were prepared, the platters on which they were served, the utensils with which they were eaten, all reflected the wealth and standing of the households, but all respected the standards and traditions of the dish, and the quality of the ingredients. Everywhere the most scrupulous and responsible care was taken of the springs, so that drinking water was always clean and safe.

From this historical introduction it is easy to see how the richness and diversification of many influences still have the power to inspire, as the chapters of this book will demonstrate. If you try to perhaps even adapt some of the recipes and suggestions in your own kitchen, then you will be joining one of the world's great historical traditions.

Afiyet olsun!

The First Turkish Cookbook

Turgut Kut

The first Turkish cookbook, Meleu't-Tabbahin, meaning 'Refuge (or Resource) of Cooks', was printed by lithography in Istanbul in August 1844, five years after the Tanzimat (political and administrative reforms of the Ottoman Empire) in 1839.

This work by Mehmed Kamil, lecturer at the medical school, was published nine times between 1844 and 1888 and consists of twelve chapters containing 227 recipes. Further recipes for salads, various sorts of *tarator* (rich sauces made with walnuts, bread, garlic, olive oil, vinegar and spices), pickles and culinary techniques, forty-six in all, were added in the margins, using measures based on the old Ottoman systems.

Mehmed Kamil had 'a desire to write a cookbook for people who love fun and pleasure'. He went on to say that, after studying old books, he had selected recipes for the most delectable and rare dishes. Publication of his book, he wrote, would 'bring relief to those who had previously had to be content with nothing but tripe soup'.

This first Turkish cookbook became the main source for other publications in later years. It was translated into English by Turabi Efendi, after traditional Turkish dishes had been served at a banquet given by the Viceroy of Egypt, Mehmet Said Pasha, for royal personages and government officials on board his yacht Fail-Jihad, moored at Woolwich, East London, in 1862.

Turabi Efendi spoke French and Arabic as well as Turkish and English, and was very close to the Khedive of Egypt, Ismail Pasha (1830–95), acting as his aide and dealing with correspondence and accounts. His wife was English, and he spent most of his time travelling to England, France and Switzerland on secret missions. He was also responsible for revised translations into Turkish of parts of the Bible.

MEZE

Stuffed Vine Leaves
Dolma
Anton Mosimann

A good dish for a *meze*, these vine-leaf parcels are popular throughout the Middle East, particularly Greece, Turkey, Lebanon and Iran. *Dolmas* to be served hot are usually made with meat; those to be served cold, with rice and flavourings only. Garnish the dish with diced tomato.

Serves 4

175g/6oz preserved vine leaves
55g/2oz/¼ cup long-grain rice
salt and freshly ground black pepper
1 medium onion, peeled and finely diced
1 tablespoon olive oil
175g/6oz lean lamb, minced
1 clove garlic, peeled and crushed
2 tablespoons fresh parsley, chopped
1 tomato, peeled, deseeded and chopped
1 teaspoon ground cinnamon
2 lemons
Tomato juice or water

To get rid of the salt, blanch the vine leaves in boiling water for about 5 minutes, then drain. Cool and separate the leaves. (If using fresh leaves, soften them in much the same way). Place the rice in a pan of water with a little salt, and bring to the boil. Simmer for about 5 minutes until the rice has softened a little, then drain and leave to cool.

Sweat the onion in the oil until softened. Drain and put into a large bowl. Add the cooled rice, the lamb, garlic, parsley, tomato and cinnamon, and season with salt and freshly ground black pepper to taste. Lay the vine leaves out on the work surface, vein side up. Place a heaped teaspoon of the filling in the centre of each leaf, fold over the sides, and roll up loosely (the rice will swell). Squeeze a little, then place the rolls in a pan with the join underneath. Pack tightly so they can't move about during cooking.

Squeeze the lemon juice over and add enough tomato juice or water to come about halfway up the *dolmas*. Cover with a lid and cook very gently on top of the stove for at least 1 hour, or until the leaves are tender. Add a little more juice or water from time to time as it is absorbed.

Serve hot or cold.

Falafel
from Hüseyin Özer's *The Sofra Cookbook*

Hüseyin Özer of Sofra calls *falafel* 'one of the most essential dishes on a tempting tray of *meze*'. He goes on:

Whether an Egyptian or a Hebrew cook first created *falafel* is a 3,000-year-old mystery, but the popularity of this vegetarian rissole or fritter throughout Turkey, the Middle East and North Africa is not in doubt. Crisp to the point of crunch on the outside, tender and well-spiced within, the irresistible *falafel* are a rich source of protein.

There are minor variations of the recipe but the core choice to make is between using chickpeas or dried white beans. At Sofra, we use both. The culinary status of the basic ingredients becomes elevated, however, once crucial flavourings are brought into play. Heady mixtures of aromatic vegetables, fresh coriander, cumin and mint lift the sturdy beans and chickpeas to dizzy heights of flavour. The important thing is to make them how you like them and call them your own.

Makes 24–28 falafel, for 6–7 people

225g/8oz/1 cup dried chickpeas, soaked in water for 12 hours
200g/7oz/1 cup dried white broad beans, soaked in water for 12 hours
3 cloves garlic, crushed
1–1½ teaspoons ground cumin
1 teaspoon ground coriander
½ teaspoon freshly ground white pepper
Salt
1 red pepper, deseeded and coarsely chopped
85g/3oz white part of leek, coarsely chopped
2 tablespoons fresh mint, finely chopped
½ Spanish onion, coarsely chopped
115g/4oz celery, destringed and finely chopped
4–5 tablespoons fresh coriander or flat-leaf parsley, finely chopped
55g/2oz spring onion, chopped
70g/2½oz/¼ cup bulgur wheat, soaked in boiling water for 15 minutes, then drained

For frying

Vegetable oil or groundnut oil
About 4 tablespoons flour (optional)

Blend the chickpeas, broad beans, garlic, cumin, ground coriander and pepper to an even, but slightly coarse, paste using a food blender. Transfer to a mixing bowl. Put all the remaining ingredients, except for the oil and flour, into the food processor and pulse for about 5–8 seconds or until they are extremely finely chopped but not yet a purée.

Using the food processor, blend the two mixtures together, in batches if necessary. Aim for a workable paste, with little pinheads of colour, which holds together when shaped into a ball. To achieve this, you may need to add a few tablespoons of water. When the consistency is right, put the mixture in the refrigerator to rest for 30 minutes.

Divide the mixture and roll into 24 to 28 balls about the size of a walnut. You can keep the shapes as balls, which are best for deep-frying, or you can flatten them into patties, which lend themselves well to being shallow-fried. A third option is to mould them into pointed dome-shapes using a special *falafel* tool. When all the *falafel* are shaped, put in refrigerator to rest for 20 minutes.

Before frying the entire batch of *falafel*, try frying just one. If the mixture does not hold together, then roll in flour. Deep-fry balls and dome-shapes for 6–8 minutes, or until crisp and deep golden-brown on the outside, cooked but tender inside. Alternatively, shallow-fry patties for 2 to 3 minutes on each side.

Remove from the oil and drain briefly on kitchen paper.

Serve hot. Possible accompaniments include tomato salad, yoghurt scattered with fresh mint or coriander, *cacık* and warm pitta bread.

Chilled Yoghurt and Cucumber Dip
Cacık
Hüseyin Özer

Cacık is a cool concoction of yoghurt and cucumber, perfumed with mint. It is best to avoid grating the cucumber unless you intend to make it hours in advance. Choose thin-skinned cucumbers leaving the skin intact for better flavour and bright appearance. Dried mint is preferable because fresh mint acquires a slightly bitter taste and a rather sad colour when in prolonged contact with yoghurt. Including garlic is optional. Properly made, *cacık* is wonderful and much more than a starter. It is a crucial element of the *meze* table and a partner for all manner of stews, pilafs, kebabs and roasts.

Serves 6–8

1 large cucumber, weighing about 500g/1lb 2oz, very finely chopped
3 tablespoons dried mint
About 2½ tablespoons olive oil
4 cloves garlic, crushed to a pulp (optional)
600ml/18fl oz/2½ cups natural yoghurt
Salt and freshly ground white pepper
A few sprigs of fresh dill
Several pinches of crushed dried chillies

Put the cucumber, dried mint and 1 tablespoon of the olive oil into a large mixing bowl. Add the garlic (if using). Add the yoghurt, stirring well. If the mixture is very stiff, add a little water, a tablespoon at a time, to loosen. Season to taste with salt and freshly ground white pepper. Chill briefly.

To serve as a starter, transfer to individual serving bowls or plates.

Garnish the centre of each with about ½ teaspoon of the remaining olive oil, a pinch of crushed dried chillies and a sprig of fresh dill.

Serve with bread. To present *cacık* as part of a *meze* table, or as an accompaniment, arrange it on a large serving plate and garnish decoratively.

Turkish Aubergine Purée
Hünkâr beğendi
Hüseyin Özer

This is an equally important member of the *meze* table because it is a 'must have' sauce for asparagus and an accompaniment for a range of kebabs; it is also a tasty starter on its own, as aubergines and cheese are well-known companions. Here they team up to form a moreish purée which is eaten with warm pitta bread, like *hummus* or *taramasalata*.

Serves 4

2 large aubergines
30g/1oz butter
6 tablespoons flour
100g/3½oz/1 cup mild English Cheddar cheese, grated
2 pinches of caster sugar
90ml/3½fl oz/¼ cup double cream
200ml/7fl oz/¾ cup milk
Salt and freshly ground white pepper
1 tablespoon fresh dill, finely chopped
A few sprigs of fresh mint
1 red pepper, cut into small diamond-shapes

Grill or roast the aubergines until the skins are charred and the flesh soft. On a wooden board, chop the aubergine flesh to form a purée, then transfer it to a bowl and set aside.

In a large saucepan, melt the butter over a medium heat. Stir in the flour to form a stiff roux. Add the grated cheese, the sugar and the double cream. With a metal balloon whisk, stir continuously until the ingredients are smoothly blended.

Add the aubergine flesh and whisk well. Gradually incorporate the milk, stirring with the whisk to avoid lumps. Taste, then season with salt and white pepper. Let the mixture bubble slightly for about 5 minutes or until it has lost its floury taste. Remove from the heat and set aside to cool slightly.

To serve as a starter, transfer warm to individual plates. Scatter with dill and garnish with mint leaves at the side of the plate. Decorate with a few diamonds of red pepper and serve straight away, with warm pitta bread.

SOUPS

Spinach Soup
Ispanak çorbası

Canan Maxton

If possible, buy the spinach from a Turkish or Greek greengrocer. It is superior in quality and will be much fresher than the supermarket offerings. Always wash the spinach before cutting it. Do not soak it in water as this will leach out all the minerals. It is best to wash it quickly and use it straight away. Thick yoghurt tastes better with this soup. Low-fat 'set' yoghurt is a possibility too.

Serves 6–8

2 bunches spinach or perpetual spinach
1 bunch fresh parsley
1 bunch fresh coriander
Small bunch fresh dill
2 tablespoons pudding rice
90g/3½oz/½ cup chickpeas, soaked and cooked, or tinned
55g/2oz butter
Salt
Plain Turkish or Greek yoghurt

Wash the spinach and the herbs, discarding only the very hard parts of the stalks. Chop reasonably finely, using a sharp knife (but not a food processor).

Put the rice in a saucepan with 565ml/1 pint/2¼ cups of water and boil for 10 minutes. Add all the other ingredients and cook until everything is soft. Add more water if you want to make it thinner, but it should not be too watery as this is a thick soup.

Serve with a tablespoonful of yoghurt in each bowl.

Fish Soup

Ali Pasiner

Serves 4–6

White or soft fish, such as scorpion fish, gurnard, sea bream or leer fish (gurnard and scorpion are best)
6 peppercorns
8 cloves garlic, finely chopped
½ glass white wine
1 green pepper, thinly sliced
Pinch salt
3 sugar cubes
1 tomato, sliced
1 whole onion
Fresh parsley, finely chopped
150g/5½oz margarine
2 potatoes, diced
2 carrots, diced.

If you've caught a large fish, for example a gurnard or sea bream, cut it into four. The remaining parts can be poached, fried or made into a *pilaki* stew.

And what if we are to use scorpion fish to make our soup? First clean the fish and remove the entrails, keeping the head on. Then cut the fish into 12 small pieces or 2 large pieces and cook in water in an open saucepan on a low heat for half an hour. It is very important to check with a fork that the fish does not become too soft.

Once the flesh begins to soften, remove fish with a slotted spoon and put on to a plate. Now add the following to the pan: 6 peppercorns, garlic, white wine, green pepper, salt, sugar, tomato, onion, parsley, margarine and a few diced potatoes and carrots. Cover the pan and cook on a medium heat until the potatoes are soft. Add the filleted fish pieces and remove the onion. Cook for a further 30 minutes over a low heat, stirring occasionally with a wooden spoon. If desired, a lemon may be squeezed into the soup after cooking.

Yoghurt

from Claudia Roden's *A New Book of Middle Eastern Food*

Milk, both fresh and sour, and particularly in the form of yoghurt, is an ancient ingredient in the cooking of the Middle East in general. In certain soups, yoghurt is added at the end of the cooking and just allowed to become hot, without boiling. In this case there is little danger of it curdling. However, when yoghurt is called for in the actual cooking, precautions must be taken to 'stabilize' it.

It is good to prepare one's own yoghurt, especially if making dishes which call for over 565ml/1 pint/2¼ cups. Besides the quite different, fresher taste, the cost will be considerably reduced.

To make yoghurt

Makes 1 pint
1 tbsp bacteria bulgaris or plain, live yoghurt
1 pint/565ml milk

If yoghurt is to be adopted as an important element in cookery, it is well worth learning how to make it at home.

All sorts of equipment has been recommended: cake tins lined with padding, feather cushions, thermometers, different-sized bottles, jars, cork tops, to name but a few. Commercial firms sell rather expensive equipment but you can do perfectly well without it. All that is needed is a large earthenware or glass bowl, a plate to cover it entirely, and a small woollen blanket (I use two shawls).

If you increase the quantity of milk, increase that of the starter (bulgaris or plain yoghurt) accordingly, but do not use too much of the latter, or the new batch of yoghurt will be excessively sour.

Bring the milk to the boil in a large pan. When the froth rises, lower

the heat and let the milk barely simmer for about 2 minutes. Turn off the heat, and allow the milk to cool to the point where you can barely dip your finger in and leave it there while you count to ten. The milk must be hot enough to sting (41–43°C /106–109°F). If the milk is much cooler or hotter than this, the yoghurt is likely to fail.

Remove any skin that has formed on the surface of the milk.

Beat the activator or plain yoghurt in a large glass or earthenware bowl until it is quite liquid. Add a few tablespoons of the hot milk, one at a time, beating vigorously between each addition. Then add the rest of the milk slowly, beating constantly until thoroughly mixed.

Cover the bowl with a large plate or with a sheet of polythene secured tightly with an elastic band. Wrap the whole bowl in a woollen blanket or shawl and leave it undisturbed in a warm place such as an airing cupboard (free of draughts) for at least 8 hours or overnight. It should be thick like a creamy custard. Do not leave the bowl in the warmth too long, or the yoghurt will become too sour.

As soon as the yoghurt is ready, you can cool it in the refrigerator. It will keep for a week, but it is preferable to make a new batch every 4 days, using some of the previous one as an activator. This will ensure a constant supply of sweet, fresh-tasting yoghurt.

To 'stabilize' yoghurt

Many Middle Eastern dishes call for yoghurt as a liquid sauce which needs to be cooked (boiled or simmered) rather than just heated. Salted goat's milk, which was used in recipes in olden times, can be cooked without curdling, which explains why medieval recipes do not give any indication of ways of preventing yoghurt from curdling. Lengthy cooking, however, causes yoghurt made with cow's milk to curdle, and stabilizers such as cornflour or egg white are required to prevent this.

You will need

1 litre/1¾ pints/4½ cups yoghurt
1 egg white, lightly beaten, or 1 tablespoon cornflour mixed with a little cold water or milk
¾ teaspoon salt

Beat the yoghurt in a large saucepan until liquid. Add the egg white, or the cornflour mixed to a light paste with water or milk, and a little salt.

Stir well with a wooden spoon. Bring to the boil slowly, stirring constantly in one direction only, then reduce the heat to as low as possible and let the yoghurt barely simmer, uncovered, for about 10 minutes, or until it has acquired a thick, rich consistency. Do not cover the pan with a lid as a drop of water falling back into the yoghurt could ruin it.

After simmering, the yoghurt can be mixed and cooked with other ingredients such as meat or vegetables with no danger of curdling.

(If carefully handled, this process can also be carried out successfully after the yoghurt has been mixed with other ingredients.)

Here are three soups in which yoghurt is added at the end of the cooking. In the third one the yoghurt is cooked with the soup.

Chicken and Barley Soup with Yoghurt
Claudia Roden

Serves 6–8

1 large onion, chopped
2 tablespoons butter
1 litre/1¾ pints/4½ cups clear chicken stock
90g/3½ oz/½ cup pearl barley, soaked in water overnight
2 tablespoons fresh parsley, finely chopped
Salt and freshly ground white pepper
1 litre/1¾ pints/4½ cups yoghurt
2 tablespoons dried mint, crushed

Fry the onion in the butter in a large saucepan until soft. Add the chicken stock (made from stock cubes if necessary) and bring to the boil.

Add the soaked and drained barley to the boiling stock and simmer over a low heat for ¾ to 1 hour, or until the barley has swelled enormously and is soft. Add the chopped parsley and season to taste with salt and freshly ground white pepper.

Beat the yoghurt in a pan. Add a little of the soup and heat vigorously. Pour the yoghurt mixture into the soup gradually, beating constantly, and heat to just below boiling point. Do not allow the soup to boil, or it will curdle.

Adjust the seasoning and serve, garnished with dried crushed mint.

Chicken and Yoghurt Soup with Rice

Claudia Roden

Serves 6–8

1 litre/1¾ pints/4½ cups chicken stock
Salt and freshly ground white pepper
55g/2oz/¼ cup rice, washed
1 litre/1¾ pints/4½ cups yoghurt
1 tablespoon cornflour, dissolved in 115ml/4fl oz/½ cup cold water
3 egg yolks, lightly beaten
2 tablespoons dried mint
2 tablespoons butter

Bring the stock, seasoned to taste, to the boil. Add the rice, reduce the heat and let it simmer while you prepare the yoghurt. In another saucepan, beat the yoghurt well and add the cornflour dissolved in water. Stir well (this will stabilize it). Add the lightly beaten egg yolks and beat again. Put the pan on the heat and bring to the boil slowly, stirring constantly in one direction. When the mixture thickens, add it slowly to the chicken and rice soup, stirring constantly, and continue to simmer gently until the rice is soft. Adjust the seasoning.

Fry the mint gently in the butter and pour a little over each individual bowl before serving.

Meat Stock Soup

Claudia Roden

Serves 6

565ml/1 pint/2¼ cups meat stock
2 tablespoons butter
1½–2 tablespoons flour
Salt and freshly ground white pepper
1 litre/1¾ pints/4½ cups yoghurt
2 tablespoons dried mint, crushed

Bring the stock to the boil in a large saucepan. Melt the butter in a small pan, add the flour and blend in well, stirring for about 5 minutes over a very low heat. Pour in a ladleful of the stock and beat well. Pour this mixture back into the stock, stirring constantly, and bring back to the boil very slowly to avoid making lumps. Cook, stirring, for 15 to 20 minutes, until the soup thickens, is very smooth, and has lost the taste of flour. Season to taste with salt and freshly ground white pepper, and remove from the heat.

Beat the yoghurt in a bowl and pour it into the soup gradually, beating vigorously. Return the pan to the heat and bring the soup to just below boiling point. Do not allow it to boil, or it will curdle.

Serve garnished with crushed dried mint.

VEGETABLES

Wicked Aubergine Pâté

from Ainsley Harriott's *In the Kitchen with Ainsley Harriott*

This is one of my wife's favourite pâtés and is always made to titillate our friends' taste-buds before the grand slam main course.

Serves 4

2 large aubergines
1 clove garlic, peeled and crushed
1 small green chilli pepper, deseeded and finely chopped
2 teaspoons lemon juice
1 tablespoon olive oil
Salt and freshly ground black pepper
Fresh parsley, chopped
Lemon wedges

Preheat the oven to 190°C/375°F/gas mark 5. Prick the aubergines all over with a fork, cut in half and place them cut-side down on a lightly greased baking sheet. Bake in preheated oven for 30 to 40 minutes until softened.

Scoop out the flesh and beat it in a food processor with the garlic, chilli and lemon juice, adding the olive oil one teaspoon at a time. Alternatively, chop the flesh of the aubergine finely and rub it through a sieve, then crush the chilli and garlic in a pestle and mortar and add to the sieved aubergine with the lemon juice. Beat well, then slowly mix in the olive oil in a steady stream until smooth.

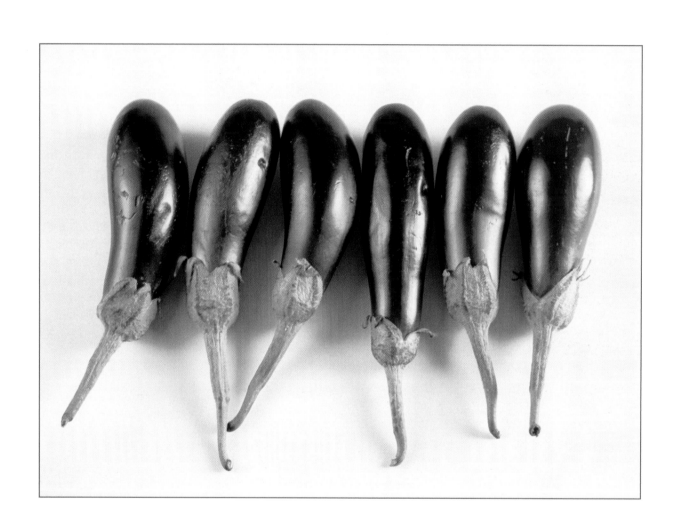

Season the pâté with salt and freshly ground black pepper to taste and stir in the parsley. Spoon on to plates or serve in ramekin dishes. Garnish with parsley and lemon wedges.

Serve with crispy toast rubbed with garlic and olive oil.

Delicate Eating

Gönül Çilasun

The abundance and variety of vegetables and fruit grown in Turkey provides a rich source of ingredients that can be used in recipes for special diets.

As well as the increasing number of vegetarians throughout the world, there are many people who prefer to have one or two meat-free days each week. Special diets recommended by dieticians include those for the common ailments diabetes and irritable bowel syndrome (IBS) as well as for lactose intolerance, low-calorie needs if slimming, nut allergies and low-protein restrictions. The award-winning Gönül Çilasun offers recipes for dishes that can be enjoyed by everybody, as starters or with a main course.

Gönül writes:

The food we all eat contains protein, one part of which (phenylalanine) cannot be broken down by persons with PKU (phenylketonuria). The foods which can be used freely are most fruits, vegetables and salads, as well as sugar, syrups, fats and vegetable oils. Many Turkish recipes, based as they are on the use of vegetables (in particular aubergines, mushrooms, peppers, tomatoes and herbs), are ideal for those with PKU and can make a colourful and varied addition to their diet.

Leeks in Olive Oil

Zeytinyağli pirasa

Gönül Çilasun

Serves 4–6

1kg/2lb 3oz trimmed leeks
2 medium carrots
2–3 tablespoons olive oil
1 tablespoon brown sugar
½ teaspoon salt
2 tablespoons regular white or special PKU rice
1–2 lemons

Chop the cleaned leeks into pieces 3–4 cm/1½–2 inches in length. Trim the carrots and chop into 0.5cm/¼ inch thick rounds. Heat the oil in a saucepan, add the leeks and carrots and cook gently, stirring, for about 5 minutes. Add the sugar, salt and rice, stir, then add 565ml/1 pint/2¼ cups of water, cover and cook slowly until the rice is tender.

Serve cold, with lots of lemon juice.

The Imam's Delight

Imam bayıldı

Gönül Çilasun

Serves 6–8

The aubergines may be fried, but it is healthier to roast them. My mother used to put in a handful of garlic cloves!

1kg/2lb 3 oz aubergines
4 tablespoons olive oil
2 large onions, halved and finely sliced
6–8 cloves garlic, sliced
2 x 400g/14oz tins chopped tomatoes

1 teaspoon cinnamon
1 tablespoon brown sugar
½ teaspoon salt
Freshly ground black pepper
285ml/½ pint/1½ cups tomato juice or water

Halve the aubergines and soak in cold water for at least 1 hour. Drain well. Using 2 tablespoons of olive oil, lightly grease a foil-covered baking tray. Lay the aubergines, flat-side down, on the tray and roast for 30 minutes, until slightly brown. While the aubergines are in the oven, heat the remaining olive oil in a pan and gently fry the onions. Add the garlic, tomatoes, cinnamon, brown sugar, salt and freshly ground black pepper. Take the aubergines from the oven, scoop out the centres with a teaspoon and fill with the onion mixture. Add the tomato juice or water and cook in a moderate oven for 30 minutes or until the aubergines are cooked.

Serve cold.

Cauliflower Salad

Karnabahar salatası

Gönül Çilasun

Serves 4–6

1 medium cauliflower
4–6 spring onions
3 sprigs fresh parsley or mint
2 tablespoons olive oil
1 dessert spoon English mustard
Juice of 1 lemon

Wash and steam the cauliflower (do not overcook). Divide into florets and place in a bowl. Chop the spring onions and the parsley or mint. Combine the olive oil, mustard and lemon juice, and add the spring onions and parsley. Pour this dressing over the cauliflower and mix well.

Serve cold.

Mixed Vegetables
Türlü
Gönül Çilasun

Serves 4–6

2 aubergines, cut into pieces
285ml/½ pint/1½ cups water
1 tablespoon sunflower oil
1 large onion, finely chopped
2 courgettes, cut into pieces
2 round red peppers, sliced
200g/7oz French beans
1 sweet potato, peeled and cut into pieces
2 x 400g/14oz tins tomatoes
3 cloves garlic, crushed
1 tablespoon olive oil
1 tablespoon brown sugar

Soak the aubergine pieces in the water for 1 hour, then drain well. Heat the oil in a large pan. Add the onions, aubergines, courgettes and peppers and fry gently until the onions begin to soften. Add the rest of the ingredients, cover the pan, and cook for 30 minutes, until the vegetables are soft (do not overcook).

Serve hot.

Mushroom Sautée
Mantar sote
Gönül Çilasun

Serves 4–6

1kg/2lb 3oz button mushrooms
Juice of 1 lemon
3 tablespoons corn oil

30g/1oz butter
1 large onion, finely chopped
1 clove of garlic
¼ teaspoon salt
Freshly ground black pepper
½ wineglass of white wine
5–6 sprigs fresh parsley

Clean the mushrooms and toss with the lemon juice. Heat the oil and butter in a pan and fry the onions and garlic until soft. Add the mushrooms, salt, freshly ground black pepper and wine, cover the pan and cook for 10 to 15 minutes on a low heat.

Serve hot, garnished with parsley.

Stuffed Tomatoes Filled with Mushrooms

Domates dolması

Gönül Çilasun

Serves 4–6

500g/1lb 2oz button mushrooms
Juice of 1 lemon
6 ripe but firm tomatoes
1 large onion
1 bunch fresh parsley
1 clove garlic
30g/1oz butter
3 tablespoons olive oil
1 tablespoon tomato purée
½ wineglass white wine

Preheat the oven to 180°C/350°F/gas mark 4. Clean the mushrooms and toss in the lemon juice. Wash the tomatoes and remove their tops. Scoop out the flesh with a teaspoon (without damaging the skins). Chop the flesh of the tomatoes into small pieces. Meanwhile, chop the onion finely and crush the garlic. Heat the butter and olive oil. Fry the onions, garlic, tomato purée and chopped tomatoes for 10 minutes, then add the mushrooms and the wine. Bring to the boil and cook for a few minutes until the mixture thickens. Fill the tomato skins with the mushroom mixture. Put one whole mushroom on top of each stuffed tomato and cook in the preheated oven for 20 minutes.

Serve hot.

Fried Courgettes in Vinegar Sauce
Sirkeli kabak kızartması
Gönül Çilasun

Serves 4–6

Make these the day before you want to serve them.

8 small courgettes
Olive oil
1 bunch fresh parsley
1 clove garlic
2 tablespoons vinegar
½ teaspoon hot chilli powder
¼ teaspoon salt

Trim the courgettes, slice into 1cm/½-inch thick ovals and cut each oval in half. Fry in a little olive oil until soft and light brown. Drain on kitchen paper to remove excess oil, and lay on a flat dish. Meanwhile, chop the parsley finely and crush the garlic. Add the vinegar, chilli and salt. Pour the mixture over the warm courgettes and leave to stand until the next day before serving.

Red Cabbage
Kırmızı lahana

Gönül Çilasun

Serves 6

2 tablespoons sunflower oil
1 medium onion, chopped
1 medium red cabbage, chopped
4 tablespoons vinegar
Salt and freshly ground black pepper

Heat the oil and fry the onion until soft. Add the cabbage and the vinegar, stir, cover the pan, and cook gently until the cabbage is tender. Season before serving.

This dish is delicious with roasted sweet potatoes.

Pepper Salad
Biber salatası

Gönül Çilasun

Serves 6

3 yellow peppers
3 red peppers
1 bunch fresh flat-leaf parsley
1 clove garlic, crushed
2 tablespoons lemon juice
2 tablespoons olive oil

Wash the peppers and halve lengthways. Roast in a hot oven or grill until the skins can be easily removed. Chop the parsley, combine with the crushed garlic and fill the peppers with this mixture. Arrange on a flat dish in alternate colours: one red 'boat', one yellow 'boat'.

Serve as a starter or salad.

Sweet Potato and Beetroot Salad

Patates ve pancar salatası

Gönül Çilasun

Serves 6

6 medium sweet potatoes
6 cooked beetroots
6 tablespoons olive oil
1 teaspoon English mustard
4 tablespoons wine vinegar
Salt
1 bunch fresh parsley, chopped
3–4 spring onions, chopped
2 tablespoons water
2 cloves garlic, crushed

Wash the sweet potatoes and cook in salted boiling water until tender.
Remove the skins and cut into rounds. Slice the beetroots. Arrange a
row of sweet potatoes and a row of beetroot on a square plate. Mix the
olive oil, mustard, vinegar, water and salt and add the parsley and spring
onions. Spoon this dressing over the potatoes and beetroot.
Serve cold.

Mixed Plate

Karışık tabak

Gönül Çilasun

Serves 6

2 carrots
¼ cauliflower
2 beetroots
2 Globe artichokes
Small bunch asparagus
1–2 sticks celery
3 tablespoons olive oil

2 tablespoons lemon juice
Salt and freshly ground black pepper
Dill, chopped

Cook each vegetable separately in salted boiling water. Cut into small pieces and arrange in circles on an oval plate: artichokes in the centre, carrots in the second row, cauliflower in the third, beetroot in the fourth, asparagus in the fifth and the celery sticks at each side.

Mix the olive oil with the lemon juice, season, and spoon over the vegetables. Sprinkle with dill.

Serve hot or cold.

Sweet Carrots
Tatlı havuç
Gönül Çilasun

Serves 6

1kg/2lb 3oz carrots
100g/3½oz butter
1 tablespoon brown sugar
565ml/1 pint/2¼ cups water
Fresh mint leaves

Preheat the oven to 190°C/375°F/gas mark 5. Scrape and wash the carrots and cut into medium rounds. Melt the butter in a pan and fry the carrots until they begin to colour, then add the sugar and water and transfer to an ovenproof dish. Roast in the preheated oven until the water is absorbed and the carrots are soft.

Sprinkle with the chopped mint and serve.

Asparagus in Olive Oil

Zeytinyalı kuşkonmaz

Gönül Çilasun

Serves 4

2–3 tablespoons olive oil
2–3 tablespoons lemon juice
1 teaspoon English mustard
Salt and freshly ground black pepper
400g/14oz asparagus

Combine the olive oil, lemon juice, mustard, salt and freshly ground black pepper to make a dressing. Wash and trim the asparagus and steam until tender. Lay the asparagus on a shallow oval plate and pour the dressing over while still warm.
  Serve cold or hot.

Stuffed Artichokes

Enginar dolması

Gönül Çilasun

Serves 4

4 fresh globe artichokes
Salt and freshly ground black pepper
2 small pickled gherkins
1 small bunch fresh parsley
1 tablespoon green olives, chopped
4 tablespoons olive oil
Juice of 1 lemon

Trim the outer leaves and the top of the artichokes and remove the choke. Cook the artichokes in boiling salted water until tender. Chop the pickled gherkins and parsley and add the green olives, olive oil,

freshly ground black pepper and lemon juice. Combine well and stuff the artichokes with this mixture.

Serve cold.

Aubergine Salad

Patlıcan salatası

Gönül Çilasun

Serves 6

4 plump aubergines, weighing 1kg/2lb 3oz
2 tablespoons olive oil
Juice of 1 lemon
1 onion
4 medium tomatoes
1 bunch fresh parsley
5 green peppers
2 tablespoons vinegar
Salt and freshly ground black pepper
Few olives

Roast the aubergines in the oven or microwave until they are soft. Remove the skin, then cut into small pieces and pour over the olive oil. Add the lemon juice to stop them turning brown. Chop the onions, tomatoes, parsley and peppers into small pieces and stir in the vinegar, salt and freshly ground black pepper. Mash the aubergines and add the onion mixture.

Decorate with olives and serve cold.

Celeriac with Mushrooms

Mantarlı kereviz

Gönül Çilasun

Serves 6

1 medium celeriac
Juice of 1 lemon
1 large onion
1 red pepper
3 tablespoons olive oil
200g/7oz button mushrooms
Salt and freshly ground black pepper
1 tablespoon brown sugar
285ml/½ pint/1½ cups water
1 bunch fresh dill

Trim the celeriac, cut into cubes and put into a bowl of water with some of the lemon juice.

Chop the onion and pepper into small pieces. Fry the onions gently in the oil until softened, then add the celeriac, peppers, mushrooms, salt, freshly ground black pepper, sugar and water and cook until the celeriac is tender.

Serve cold, sprinkled with chopped dill and lemon juice.

White Cabbage with Button Mushrooms

Mantarlı beyaz lahana

Gönül Çilasun

Serves 6

1 medium cabbage, weighing 1kg/2lb 3oz
1 large onion
4 tablespoons sunflower oil
1 teaspoon fresh chillies, chopped

Salt
300g/11oz button mushrooms
565ml/1 pint/2¼ cups water

Chop the cabbage and onion. Fry the onion gently in the oil until softened, then add the cabbage, chillies and salt. Cook for a few minutes, then add the mushrooms and cook for another 5 to 6 minutes.

Serve hot or cold.

Vegetarian Goulash
Sebzeli gulaş
Gönül Çilasun

Serves 6

2 tablespoons olive oil
2 medium onions, sliced
1 heaped tablespoon paprika
Several pinches of cayenne pepper
1 x 400g/14oz tin Italian tomatoes
565ml/1 pint/2¼ cups tomato juice
½ cauliflower, cut into florets
255g/9oz carrots
255g/9oz sweet potatoes
1 green pepper, deseeded and chopped
Salt and freshly ground black pepper

Preheat the oven to 180°C/350°F/gas mark 4.

Heat the oil in a large ovenproof pan and fry the onions until softened. Add most of the paprika and the cayenne pepper. Cook for a few minutes, then stir in the tomatoes and tomato juice. Bring to the boil, stirring all the time, then add all the vegetables.

Season with salt and freshly ground black pepper, cover the pan, transfer to the preheated oven and bake for 30 to 40 minutes.

Sprinkle with the remainder of the paprika and serve.

Roasted Vegetables in Yoghurt

Jane Whiter, Chef, Westminster Classic Tours

Serves

2 tomatoes
4 courgettes
1 red pepper
1 green pepper
1 large or 2 small aubergines
2 tablespoons olive oil
1 clove garlic
½ litre natural yoghurt
Salt and freshly ground black pepper

Quarter the tomatoes and divide the courgettes in four lengthways. Quarter the peppers and remove the cores. Cut the aubergines into thick slices. Place all the vegetables in a bowl, sprinkle with the olive oil and leave for an hour or so.

Preheat the oven to 190°C/375°F/gas mark 5. Transfer the vegetables to a baking tray and roast in the preheated oven for an hour. Crush the garlic with a little salt and add it to the yoghurt, then pour over the roasted vegetables when they are cool. Sprinkle with red pepper flakes or paprika. You can add cooked potatoes to this if you like.

Turkish Spinach

Berrin Torolsan

The sweetmeat of kings, the fuel of warriors, spinach is bursting with colour, vitality and flavour.

Spinach has been in cultivation since remote times in Anatolia and has many wild, semi-wild and cultivated forms. It is known in the countryside as *can otu*: 'life green'. It was recommended by the physician Hizir Pasa in the fifteenth century in his book of medicines as being 'cooling and digestive and exceedingly good sustenance'. Folklore and modern medicine confirm his wisdom.

An illustration of the enthusiasm felt over the years by cooks for spinach comes from a Turkish cookery book written in 1943 by Bahri Özdeniz:

'My dear mother washes her spinach leaves with her saintly white hands in several changes of water then leaves them to drain in a colander, all nicely chopped. Humming the tune of an old song, she finely chops an onion, lights the stove, wipes clean her pan once more and heats some of her delicious-smelling fat and adds the spinach and onion, stirring gently with a wooden spoon as she lightly fries them. She then mixes a crushed clove of garlic and salt into thick creamy yoghurt and pours it over the spinach. I used to jump with excitement when this dish arrived at the table. Prepared like this, spinach adds life to one's life ...'

Bahri Özdeniz's book is not a manual for cooking, nor is it selling anything. It is all about the sheer love of food.

In preparation, spinach requires kindness to preserve flavour and goodness; it should be simmered briefly or gently stir-fried and it is better to undercook. Don't blanch except if you are making spinach purée. Using too many ingredients, devilling with hot spices or adding heavy, rich sauces, interferes with the benevolence of spinach. A light touch and affection should be the main ingredients. The reward will be yours to enjoy.

Spinach with Eggs
Ispanaklı yumurta
Berrin Torolsan

Even without eggs, sautéd spinach, or ispanak kavurmasi, is a dish in its own right, listed in the fifteenth-century Topkapı Palace kitchen records.

Serves 2–4

255g/9oz spinach
1 tablespoon butter
1 onion, finely chopped
Salt and freshly ground black pepper
Pinch of sugar
2 eggs

Wash, drain and shred the spinach. Melt the butter in a frying pan and sauté the onion until it is translucent and soft but not caramelized. Add the spinach, a small amount at a time, and stir-fry until wilted and reduced in volume. Season with salt, freshly ground black pepper and the sugar.

With the back of a spoon make two hollows in the centre of the spinach and break an egg into each. Cover the pan and cook on a gentle heat for a further two minutes, until the egg whites are set and the yolks clouded.

Serve with oven-fresh bread.

Spinach with Onions

Soğanlı ispanak

Berrin Torolsan

Serves 4–6

This vegetarian dish is delicious served with garlicky yoghurt.

2 tablespoons corn or olive oil
1 large onion, finely chopped
1kg/2lb 3oz spinach, washed thoroughly
½ teaspoon salt
½ teaspoon freshly ground black pepper

Heat the oil in a saucepan and fry the onions gently until soft. Add the spinach, salt and freshly ground black pepper and stir gently for 5 minutes.

Serve hot or cold.

FISH

The Turkish Sea Harvest
Ali Pasiner

Throughout history Istanbul has been famous for its fish. Western travellers have rightly praised it for its fish restaurants and the opportunities it offers to buy the very best. During Ottoman times, rich industrialist families along the Bosphorus and its islands used to eat fish and seafood, although the majority of people considered it unclean because it was said that fish was killed without the flow of blood.

The specialist fish chefs for the great banquets paid great attention to aesthetic presentation. When a gentleman gave a dinner party at his waterside residence, the chef would bring in the 4-kilo sea bass on a great platter, to the satisfaction of the host. At exclusive Bosphorus dinner tables it was considered appropriate to serve sea bass, swordfish, gurnard, bluefish, grey mullet and turbot. For the residents of the islands, on the other hand, the most esteemed dishes were red sea bass, sea bream, scorpion fish, and especially sur and striped red mullet. In recent times lobster, swordfish, tuna and mackerel have come to grace the tables of the poor.

The Turkish Kitchen Club describes ten ways of cooking pilaf, thirty types of *börek* and at least forty aubergine dishes, but only a few ways to cook fish. Unfortunately, our outlook has always been more towards the land than the sea, so we have not developed the cooking techniques or accorded the produce of the sea the place it deserves.

At the best dinner parties along the Bosphorus, special tables are set with a variety of fish dishes and other seafood where the masters proudly show off their elaborate fare. Fish will include tuna, grey mullet,

bluefish, atherine, gurnard, striped red mullet, along with sun-dried mackerel, salted tuna, tuna fishcakes, smoked bluefish and mackerel, salted sea bream, prawn salad, prawn and bean stew, prawn pilaf, prawn and cheese casserole, fried mussels, mussel salad and stew (pilaki), crab casserole, boiled crab, scorpion fish, fish soup or stew. These fish will be poached, fried or grilled in the oven. For some reason dishes made with bluefish have generally been grilled, although at the banquets of Sultan Hamit one of the *meze* would be made with the boiled cheek of the large bluefish, made into a delicious salad with olive oil, lemon juice, black pepper, salt, garlic and parsley.

Salted Fish

Tuzlu balık

Ali Pasiner

Serves 4–6

1 bluefish
2 teaspoons sea salt
2 teaspoons whole black peppercorns
Bunch bay leaves
Olive oil
1 lemon

Salted bluefish is exceptionally delicious, and here is a recipe for a special *meze*. First clean a large fish and take off the head. Then slice down the belly and remove the spine. Put some sea salt in a large tin and add the fish in layers, interspersed with more salt, whole black peppercorns and bay leaves. Put a lid on the tin, place a large weight on top and seal. After 15 days, remove and wash the fish and hang by the tail in the sunniest and windiest corner of the garden. Within 10 days oil will ooze out and the fish will become yellowish. Now collect the fish, place it under running water and skin it. Drizzle with olive oil and lemon juice and serve.

Poaching

Poaching is generally used for hard, scaly white fish such as sea bream, red sea bream, black-eyed sea bream and sea bass. Wash and clean the fish under running water, then lay it on a surface lined with newspaper. Descale using a spoon – this way you will avoid splashing and making a mess.

Poached Sea Bream
Mercan buğulama
Ali Pasiner

Serves 4–6

1 sea bream
3 tomatoes, peeled and sliced
1 chilli pepper
6 cloves garlic
2 sugar cubes
115ml/4fl oz/½ cup white wine
2oz butter
Salt and pepper

Now let's look at how to poach sea bream. After the fish is descaled, place it on a tray and cover with peeled and sliced tomatoes. Score both sides of the fish two or three times, depending on the size of the fish. Next, push a knob of butter into the inside of the fish and into each of the score cuts. Sprinkle both sides with black peppercorns.

Push knobs of butter into the corners of the tray. Add more peeled and sliced tomatoes to cover the fish, and place thinly sliced chilli pepper and garlic on top. Now melt sugar cubes in the white wine and pour this mixture over the fish. Season with salt and freshly ground black pepper and cover the tomatoes with parsley and bay leaves. Note that up to now we have not added any lemon, water or onion. The tomatoes will provide all the juices needed. Onion and lemon would ruin the taste of the fish.

Once the dish is prepared it should be covered, and needs to cook for 15 to 20 minutes on a medium heat. After this, lower the heat for a further 10 minutes to ensure the bottom does not overcook (make sure you keep the lid on during cooking).

Stuffed Mussels

Midye dolması

Ali Pasiner

Serves 4–6

100 mussels
1½ glassfuls of rice
6–7 large onions
1 tumbler of olive oil
1 dessert spoon salt
2 tablespoons pinenuts
2 tumblers water
1 tablespoon currants
1 soup spoon sugar
1 dessert spoon paprika
1 teaspoon cinnamon
Freshly ground black pepper
1 medium cabbage
Sardines

Stuffed mussels are delicious, and with their black shiny shells they look very attractive displayed on a plate. Then there are stuffed mussels made with cabbage, a dish which looks like normal stuffed cabbage but tastes even better.

Clean the mussels; then take the rice, wash it and sieve it. Next chop the onions and put them into a saucepan with the olive oil, salt and pinenuts, and stir over a medium heat until golden brown. Add the mussels and stir slowly without adding any water. As soon as the liquid reduces, add the rice and stir for a further 10–15 minutes. At this stage add the water, currants and sugar and leave to cook.

Once the liquid reduces, remove the pan from the heat. Add the

paprika, cinnamon, and a pinch of freshly ground black pepper, stir and leave to cool. Wash a medium cabbage from which the root has been removed with a knife. Place the cabbage in a saucepan with the stalk end downwards. Add some salt, and enough water to cover, then put the lid on the pan and boil until the leaves are soft. Transfer the cabbage to a colander and leave to cool. Next, remove the leaves carefully and cut out the veins with a knife. Place 2 or 3 mussels in the middle of each leaf and either roll into finger shapes or wrap into squares. Line the bottom of a saucepan with the outer leaves and put the stuffed mussels on top, followed by a layer of sardines. On the very top place the remainder of the leaves and add one tumblerful of water. To stop the cabbage rolls bursting, place a plate on top to weigh them down and then put the lid on the pan. Finally, cook over a slow heat until the liquid is reduced. Serve cold, sprinkled with lemon juice.

Tuna Patties

Ton balığı koftesi

Ali Pasiner

Serves 6

2 tuna (about 1lb each)
3–4 eggs
Bread
3 onions
1 dessert spoon granulated sugar
2 teaspoons salt
1 Turkish cup mixed nuts
Raisins to taste
1 tablespoon paprika
Freshly ground black pepper
Olive oil
Lemon juice

Remove heads and tails from fish. Divide into three pieces and wash well. Place in a saucepan with enough water to cover, and boil for 15 minutes with the lid on.

Take out the cooked fish with a slotted spoon and remove the black skin and the bones. Put the fish into a deep bowl. Add 3 or 4 eggs, and some soaked and squeezed bread that has had the crusts removed. Then grate the onions into this mixture, together with sugar and salt, and knead thoroughly. Next add nuts, raisins, freshly ground black pepper and a spoonful of paprika and knead until the whole mixture becomes dough-like.

Roll the mixture into finger or round shapes, making sure the nuts and raisins do not fall out. Fry the patties in hot olive oil – if you like you can first roll them in flour or cornflour.

Serve hot or cold, with a sprinkle of lemon juice.

Paper-wrapped Fish Kebabs

Ali Pasiner

Serves 6

1 sea bass
2 teaspoonfuls salt
2–3 onions
Bunch parsley, finely chopped
3 tomatoes
4–5 fresh chillies
Olive oil

First remove the scales, head, gills and tail. Split the belly and clean out the fish. Fillet both sides by cutting away at the spine. Separate the upper ribs, wash and leave to drain on one side.

Next rub salt into the onions, thinly sliced into half-rings, and add chopped parsley. Drop tomatoes into boiling water and remove after half a minute (boiling makes it very easy to peel the tomatoes, which are then sliced and deseeded). Next, divide the chillies into three.

Now oil 2 sheets of A4 greaseproof paper with olive oil and sprinkle onto this a little of the onion mixture. Put the two pieces of filleted fish on top, followed by more of the onion mixture. Add 3 or 4 slices of tomato and chilli, and drizzle with a little olive oil. Grease the tray lightly with olive oil to prevent sticking. Dampen the edges of the greaseproof paper to seal, put them back on the baking tray, and cook for 30 to 40 minutes.

Do's and Don'ts when Cooking Fish
Ali Pasiner

Don't

- Buy fish that's soft, with sunken eyes or gills that are pink, not red
- Keep fish in the fridge for too long
- Use a blunt knife when cleaning fish
- Add lemon while cooking fish
- Lift the lid too often when poaching
- Attempt to gut fish such as scorpion fish that have poisonous spines – leave this to your fishmonger

Do

- Eat fish in season
- Use newspaper on worktops when cleaning fish
- Use a spoon, not a knife, to remove scales. This way you will avoid the scales splashing all over the kitchen
- Wash fish with plenty of water before cooking, then leave in a colander for 10 to 15 minutes to drain well
- Before frying fish, salt it and let it rest for a few minutes. Before rolling it in flour and frying, sprinkle with a little *rakı*
- Fry fish in very hot oil. Drop in a piece of bread – if it bubbles the oil is hot enough
- When frying, place separate pieces of fish side by side but not touching
- Wash your hands in lemon juice diluted with water to remove any fishy smells

Turkish Stuffed Mussels with Egg and Lemon Sauce

Terbiye soslu Türk midyesi

Richard Cawley

Serves 4–6

1 tablespoon olive oil
1 onion, peeled and chopped
1 clove garlic, peeled and crushed
30g/1oz pinenuts
30g/1oz currants
55g/2oz/¼ cup long-grain rice
3 tablespoons fresh parsley, chopped
285ml/½ pint/1½ cups chicken or vegetable stock
Salt and freshly ground black pepper
48 live mussels, cleaned and opened, but left in shells
565ml/1 pint/2¼ cups water
2 egg yolks
Juice of 1 lemon

Heat the oil in a saucepan and fry the onion until transparent. Add the garlic, pinenuts, currants, rice and 1 tablespoon of parsley. Cook, stirring, for 1 minute. Pour over the stock just to cover. Cover the pan tightly and cook over a very low heat until all the water is absorbed and the rice is tender. Cool and season to taste with salt and freshly ground black pepper.

Divide the rice mixture between the mussels, pressing it into the empty half of each shell. Close and tie each shell firmly shut with thin string or cotton thread.

Pack the mussels closely together in a medium saucepan. Pour over the water. Bring to the boil, then cover and simmer gently for 30 minutes.

Take the mussels out of the pan using a slotted spoon. Remove the strings and keep the mussels warm. Mix the egg yolks with the lemon juice and add to the liquid in the pan. Heat, whisking constantly, until the sauce thickens – do not allow it to boil or the eggs will scramble. Add the remaining parsley and season to taste with salt and freshly ground black pepper.

Drunken Fish and Hidden Fish
Feride Alp

Fish and bread are symbols of fertility in Islam, and Turkey, being surrounded by seas on three sides and also being a nation of bread-lovers, certainly has the census figures to show for it. Gone are the days when you could buy your fish from fishermen passing underneath the window of your *yali* on the Bosphorus, but there is still plenty of fresh and tasty fish to be enjoyed in Turkey. Here are two recipes to be accompanied with lots of fresh bread.

Drunken Fish
Sarhoş balık
Feride Alp

Cooking with wine is not common in Turkey; *rakı* would be used instead. This recipe comes from the Aegean region and is both quick and easy to prepare.

Serves 4–6

2 red onions
6 cloves garlic, crushed with salt
3 tablespoons olive oil
1kg/2lb 3oz any kind of fish, including squid
285ml/½ pint/1½ cups white wine or 140ml/¼ pint/just over ½ cup *rakı*
Juice of ½ lemon
½ teaspoon mustard
Salt and freshly ground black pepper
1 large bunch fresh parsley, coarsely chopped

Brown the onions and garlic in the oil. Add the fish and all the other

ingredients except for the parsley. Cover and cook over a gentle heat for 10 to 15 minutes. Toss in the parsley and serve.

Hidden Fish

Gizli balık

Feride Alp

This method of baking with coarse sea salt results in a wonderfully tender fish. The salt is not absorbed.

Serves 4

1 fish, weighing 1–1½ kg/2lb 3oz–3½ lb, e.g. sea bass, sea bream or salmon (*levrek*)
1 egg white
Sea salt
Slices of lemon
Olive oil

Preheat the oven to 190°C/375°F/gas mark 5.

Wash and gut the fish, leaving it whole. Mix the egg white with sea salt. Cover the bottom of an ovenproof dish with a thick layer of salt, put the fish on top and cover completely with another thick layer of salt so as to seal the fish. Bake in the preheated oven for about 1 hour. Bring to the table and crack the salt with a knife. Remove the top layer of salt – the skin of the fish may come off with it.

Serve with lemon slices and olive oil.

Freshwater Trout

Alabalık

Antony Worrall Thompson

Freshwater fish has become rather unfashionable. It wasn't that long ago that every restaurant menu included trout, but where has it gone? The question should actually be: where has the flavour gone? Since the introduction of farmed trout, brown trout and true rainbow trout have disappeared from local rivers, to a large extent because of pollution.

In Britain there's not much choice of freshwater fish in a culinary sense. In a nation where fishing is a major hobby it is rare to see perch, carp and roach finding their way on to our plates, yet other European countries have recipes for all of them. If you are ever in Switzerland or France, try *omble-chevalier*, which is lake char or Arctic char – truly delicious. In Britain we are really limited to trout, salmon, crayfish, pike and eel. And it is disputable whether or not salmon is actually a river fish, as most of it is farmed at sea. Even wild salmon is often trapped in estuaries as they attempt to make their way up their home rivers to spawn.

With the demise of the fishmonger one will rarely, if ever, see eel or pike on the slab. I have seen 'golden trout' in supermarkets, something that didn't really impress me with its flavour.

Fish of any kind has to be really fresh to fully reveal its delicious flavour. Look for glossy, shiny skin, bright full eyes and bright red gills. Ask your fishmonger to clean and fillet the fish for you – he's the expert, and will be delighted to do it.

For this recipe, ask your fishmonger to 'spatchcock' the trout by cutting a slit through the belly and removing the backbone. The trout is then opened out to create a large flat area which is spread with a purée of roasted peppers.

Serves 4

3 roasted red peppers, quartered, seeded and skinned
85g/3oz/½ cup toasted pinenuts
85g/3 oz/1½ cups fresh breadcrumbs
3 cloves garlic, finely chopped
2 tablespoons extra virgin olive oil
Salt and freshly ground black pepper

Olive oil for the pan
4 'spatchcocked' trout

Place the peppers in a food processor and blend until smooth. Add the pinenuts, breadcrumbs and garlic and blend again to a smooth purée. With the machine running, add the olive oil in a thin stream. Season with salt and freshly ground black pepper. Slash the skin of the trout. Rub the fish on the flesh side with the red pepper purée and push some purée into the slashes as well. Refrigerate for 30 minutes.

Heat a ridged griddle pan, large frying pan or barbecue until very hot. Oil the pan or the grill bars of the barbecue and cook the trout, flesh side down, for 3 minutes. Turn the fish carefully and repeat. Transfer to a serving platter.

Serve with buttered noodles, rice or new potatoes.

MEAT

Lamb Shanks with Aubergine
Incik

Sami Zubaida

Serves 4

4 lamb shanks or knuckles (shanks are from the leg and are larger, knuckles from the shoulder)
Salt and freshly ground black pepper
2 onions, chopped
Oil for frying
Ground allspice (1 or 2 teaspoons)
Ground cumin (1 or 2 teaspoons; optional)
½ teaspoon sugar
1 tablespoon tomato purée
Dash of vinegar or Worcester sauce
285ml/½ pint/1½ cups water or stock
2 medium to large aubergines

Preheat the oven to 180°C/350°F/gas mark 4. Brown the lamb shanks on all sides in hot oil, season with salt and pepper, and transfer to an oven tray. In the same pan soften the onions in oil. Add the spices and fry for 1 minute, then add the sugar, tomato purée and vinegar. Add the water or stock and stir well. Pour this mixture over the meat and cover with foil. Bake in the preheated oven until tender (1 to 2 hours, depending on the quality of the meat and the size of the shanks).

Cut the aubergine into slices lengthwise, sprinkle with salt and leave to stand for 20 minutes. Wash off the salt and juices and pat dry. Fry the slices in oil until soft, but don't let them disintegrate. Drain on kitchen paper.

Remove the meat from the oven, take off the foil and add the aubergines. Spoon the sauce over the top and return to the oven for 20 minutes.

Stuffing Rice
İç pilavi
Sami Zubaida

Now served as a dish in its own right, this type of rice resembles Italian risotto or Spanish paella rice, but the long-grain rice commonly used now will do just as well for this recipe.

Serves 4–6

300g/11oz/1½ cups rice
Butter, preferably clarified, and/or oil for frying
Salt and freshly ground black pepper
Water or stock to cover
30g/1oz pinenuts, and/or chopped almonds
20g/¾oz raisins (optional)
1 onion, finely chopped
6 chicken livers or 255g/9oz lamb's liver
Allspice
Fresh parsley and/or dill, chopped
Extra butter for oven

Soak the rice in warm water for an hour (longer does no harm) and drain. Toss the rice in hot butter or oil in a heavy saucepan to coat the grains. Add salt, cover with water or stock, bring to the boil and cook until the liquid is absorbed. Cover the pan with a cloth and a lid and allow to steam over a low flame for 20 minutes.

In a frying pan fry the nuts until they colour, add the raisins (if used), then remove and reserve. Add a little more butter or oil to the pan and soften the chopped onion, then add the roughly chopped liver, a little salt, freshly ground black pepper and allspice, and cook for a few minutes. Add this mixture to the rice, mix well and add the herbs. Leave over a low flame for a further 10 to 15 minutes, or transfer to a heated oven dish, dot with bits of butter on the surface and bake in a moderate oven for 15 minutes.

In one market restaurant in an Aegean town, I was served *iç pilavi* which had been finished in the oven covered with a sheet of caul fat, which had crisped and melted into the rice. Sumptuous.

Pera Palas Pie
Josceline Dimbleby

I first went to Turkey at the age of eighteen, travelling on one of the last journeys of the original Orient Express from Paris. My girlfriend's wealthy father was paying for our trip and on arrival in Istanbul we went to the legendary spies' hotel, the Pera Palas. It was certainly a hotel to capture our imagination, with its much faded grandeur: huge and shabby reception rooms, marble floored bathrooms and ornate, gilded lift. The hotel was almost empty when we stayed there, and I shall always remember our first evening when the two of us sat completely alone in the palatial dining room, with a neat row of waiters staring at us curiously from the far end of the room.

Until that meal, I had always thought of dill as a Scandinavian herb, and pine kernels as something characteristically Lebanese. In Istanbul, however, you will find fresh dill and pinenuts mixed with rice, lamb and fish. In this dish I have used them to make an exceptionally good type of *moussaka* with a Turkish flavour. The aubergine is surely to Turkey what the leek is to Wales, and the smooth cheese topping of this dish is dotted with pieces of aubergine and toasted pinenuts. I serve it with rice and a green salad or vegetable, and to make it more substantial I sometimes put a layer of sliced cooked potatoes between the meat and the topping.

Serves 4–6

1 large aubergine, weighing about 340g/12oz
Lemon juice or white wine vinegar

Salt and freshly ground black pepper
3 tablespoons olive oil
30g/1oz pinenuts, plus a few extra
500g/1lb 2oz lean minced lamb
2 cloves garlic, finely chopped
2 teaspoons paprika
2 tablespoons chopped fresh dill or 3 teaspoons dried dill
55g/2oz plain flour
565ml/1 pint/2¼ cups milk
255g/9oz soft white cheese

Cut the unpeeled aubergine into 1cm/½ inch slices and smear all over with the lemon juice or vinegar. Then rub the slices with salt and leave in a colander in the sink for 30 minutes. Preheat the oven to 190°C/375°F/gas mark 5.

Rinse the slices well, dry with kitchen paper and cut into small cubes. Heat 2 tablespoons of olive oil in a large frying pan over a high heat, add the aubergines and stir for a few minutes until soft and browned. Transfer to a plate. Now add the pinenuts to the pan, stir for a minute or two until browned, then remove to another plate. Heat the remaining tablespoon of oil in the frying pan over a fairly high heat. Add the minced lamb and fry, breaking up the meat, for a few minutes until any liquid has evaporated and the meat has browned. Add the chopped garlic and the paprika, cook for another minute or two and then remove the pan from the heat. Stir in the chopped dill and empty the meat into a shallow, ovenproof dish.

To make the topping, put the flour into a saucepan away from the heat and stir in a little of the milk with a wooden spoon until you have a smooth paste. Stir in the remaining milk and bring to the boil, stirring all the time. Let it bubble, still stirring, for 2 to 3 minutes, then remove the pan from the heat, add the cheese and stir or whisk thoroughly until blended into the sauce. Season to taste with salt and freshly ground black pepper. Stir in the reserved fried aubergines and pinenuts and pour the sauce over the lamb in the dish. Scatter a few more unbrowned pinenuts on top. Cook the pie towards the top of the preheated oven for about 30 minutes, until it has browned on top.

Macaroni and Meat Pie

Pastitchio

from Chez Nico Restaurants

Nico Ladenis

Serves 4–6

500g/1lb 2oz long macaroni
1 onion, chopped
A little olive oil
500g/1lb 2oz lean minced beef
1.7 litres/3 pints/7½ cups béchamel sauce, flavoured with Gruyère cheese
and nutmeg
2 tablespoons tomato purée
225ml/8fl oz/1 cup passata
225ml/8fl oz/1 cup chicken stock
Salt and freshly ground black pepper
Ground cinnamon
2 sugar cubes
Butter
Gruyère cheese for topping

Béchamel sauce

70 g butter
70 g flour
1 litre milk
Salt
Cayenne pepper
Nutmeg

Cook the macaroni in plenty of boiling salted water until *al dente*. Drain
and put to one side.

Gently fry the chopped onion in a little olive oil, add the meat and
cook until slightly browned and dry. Add the tomato purée, passata,
chicken stock, salt, pepper and cinnamon (and a little sugar if necessary).
Simmer for about 20 minutes or until all the liquid is absorbed.

Preheat the oven to 180°C/350°F/gas mark 4. Soak the macaroni in
béchamel sauce for a couple of hours. Spoon half the macaroni into a large

baking tray, spreading along the bottom. Spread the minced meat evenly on top of the macaroni and cover with the remainder of the macaroni.

Pour over the remainder of the béchamel and sprinkle with small knobs of butter and a little more cheese.

Bake in the preheated oven until golden brown.

Hummus with Seared Lamb and Toasted Pinenuts

Kavurmalı ve fıstıklı hummus

from Nigella Lawson's *How to Eat*

Nigella writes: This isn't an obvious pairing, but I think it's an authentic one. That's to say, although I've never seen mention of it in cookery books, I've eaten it – in both Turkish and Lebanese restaurants. And I love this combination of cold, thickly nutty, buff-coloured paste and hot, lemony-sweet shards of meat, and the waxy, resiny nuts: it instantly elevates the *hummus* from its familiar deli-counter incarnation. You could use good bought *hummus* – but just dribble a little good olive oil on top, and around the edges, before topping with the nuts and lamb.

As far as authenticity goes, I don't make any claims for my *hummus* recipe: for I add Greek yoghurt. Nor do I apologize for my innovation. Home-made *hummus* can be stodgy and cloggy, and I love the tender whippedness that you get in restaurant versions (which, come to think of it, are probably bought in). If you leave out the Greek yoghurt, you may have to add a little more of the chickpea cooking liquid. Don't be afraid of making this too liquid; it'll most likely stiffen on keeping anyway. With the yoghurt, I find I can still use up to 200ml/7fl oz/1 cup of cooking liquid when puréeing the chickpeas.

I buy noisettes of lamb here, because I know that, once I've stripped off the encircling fat, they'll be lean but still satiny within. If pressed, I suppose you could buy those little rags of meat carved ready for stir-frying from the supermarket – just make sure you cut each little piece in half again. Think of lardons, then imagine them cut in half horizontally: that's the size of meat strip you're aiming for.

Serves 4–6

300g/11oz/2 cups dried chickpeas, soaked in water overnight
1 onion, whole but peeled
2 bay leaves
7 cloves garlic: 3 unpeeled, 4 peeled
3 tablespoons olive oil
Salt and freshly ground black pepper
9 tablespoons *tahina*
2–3 lemons
A large pinch of ground cumin
3–5 tablespoons Greek yoghurt
325g/12oz lean, tender lamb
75g/2½oz/½ cup pinenuts
3 tablespoons garlic-infused or plain olive oil
Fresh flat-leaf parsley, chopped

Drain the chickpeas, cover with fresh water, and simmer until cooked, throwing the onion, bay leaves and 3 unpeeled cloves of garlic into the pot too. It is imperative you taste the chickpeas before draining to test that they are truly cooked: undercooked chickpeas make for an unsatisfactorily grainy texture and you want a voluptuous velvetiness here, no hard surfaces. When you're satisfied the chickpeas are buttery and tender, dunk a mug in to catch a good 350 ml/12fl oz/2 cups of the cooking liquid, and then you can drain the chickpeas with a clear conscience.

In the bowl of a food processor fitted with the double-bladed knife, put the peeled cloves of garlic, roughly chopped, a teaspoon of salt, 100ml/4fl oz/½ cup of the cooking liquid, 3 tablespoons of olive oil, the *tahina*, the juice of 1 lemon and the cumin. Blitz until well and truly puréed. Taste, adding more liquid as you feel you need to slacken and soften the mixture. Process again, then grind in some black pepper, adding 3 dolloping tablespoons of Greek yoghurt and give another whizz. Taste to see whether you want to add any more lemon juice (and you could want double) or Greek yoghurt, or indeed oil or seasoning. When you have a smooth yet dense purée with the intensity you like, scrape out into a bowl, cover. and keep in the fridge until about an hour before you want to eat it.

You can toast the pinenuts before then, but the lamb must be done at the last minute. To be frank, then, you may as well do them both together. Cut the lamb into tiny, thin shreds – little rags and tatters of meat – and decant the *hummus* into a shallow round or oval bowl. Put both to one side for a moment.

Put a heavy-based frying pan on the hob over medium heat, add the pinenuts and shake every so often until they begin to take on a deep golden colour and their resiny fragrance rises from the pan. Transfer to a plate or bowl, and then add the rest of the oil to the pan. I often use garlic-infused oil here because I like it when the lamb has a garlicky taste, but I don't want burnt shards of garlic mixed up with it. Marinating with a few cloves of crushed garlic can work, but then the lamb doesn't sear as well. But ordinary olive oil works well too, and because the *hummus* itself is garlicky, you hardly risk blandness by omitting the garlic with the lamb.

When whichever oil you are using is hot in the pan, toss in the lamb and stir furiously until it begins to crisp and brown at the edges. Hold half a lemon over the pan and give a good hard squeeze. Push the meat about once more and empty the contents of the pan evenly over the *hummus*, lemony oil juices and all. Sprinkle with, preferably, coarse salt, grind over some black pepper and scatter with the toasted pinenuts. Add some freshly chopped parsley, then serve immediately and with lots of oven-warmed pitta.

PILAF & PULSES

Cracked Wheat Salad

from Sally Clarke's Recipes from a Restaurateur, Shop and Bakery

I've never understood why every cracked wheat salad recipe calls for first soaking the wheat in water. Presumably, it's traditionally correct to do so – this is a simple dish, after all. But what is more tasteless than water? Instead, at the restaurant, I make a pungent, spicy and flavourful juice out of the skins and seeds of the tomatoes. I believe this is what makes our cracked wheat salad the best. (It improves – if that's possible – with keeping for a day or so.)

Serves 6–8

680g/1½lb firm but ripe tomatoes
1 cucumber
1 bunch fresh basil, stalks and leaves separated
¼ bunch of fresh mint, stalks and leaves separated
1 bunch fresh coriander, stalks and leaves separated
½ bunch fresh parsley, stalks and leaves separated
½ bunch fresh chives, finely chopped
400g/14oz overripe tomatoes
1 fresh red chilli, deseeded
Juice of 2–3 large lemons
2 cloves garlic
2 teaspoons Maldon salt

255g/9oz/1¼ cups cracked wheat
Approximately 90ml/3½fl oz/a cup good olive oil

Plunge the firm tomatoes into boiling water, leave for 3 seconds and remove them to a bowl of iced water. Peel, quarter and deseed, keeping all the skins, juice and seeds in a bowl. Neatly dice the flesh of the tomatoes.

Cut the cucumber in half, lengthwise, and scoop out the seeds, adding them to the tomato seeds. Dice the cucumber and add to the tomato. Roughly chop the basil, mint, coriander and parsley leaves and toss gently into the tomato salad with the chives. Cover and refrigerate.

Liquidize the tomato seeds and skins with the overripe tomatoes, chilli, the juice of 2 of the lemons, garlic, herb stalks and salt and pass through a sieve, pushing the debris with a ladle to extract all the juice. Check for seasoning – it should taste salty and spicy. Place the cracked wheat in a bowl and pour in three-quarters of the liquid. Stir well and leave to soak for at least 1 hour in a cool place. Stir again, adding the remaining liquid and some of the olive oil. It should look and feel moist, though not runny. Leave for another 30 minutes, then gently fold in the tomato salad.

Add more lemon juice, olive oil and salt to taste, and serve.

Carrot and Spinach Pilaf
Roz Denny

Serves 4

255g/9oz/1¼ cups easy-cook basmati rice
1 onion, chopped
½ small aubergine, chopped
2 cloves garlic, crushed
2 tablespoons sunflower oil
30g/1oz butter
1–2 tablespoons *garam masala*
2 carrots, grated coarsely
1 litre/1¾ pints/4½ cups vegetable stock
Sea salt and freshly ground black pepper
115g/4oz baby spinach leaves
55g/2oz/a cup unsalted cashew nuts, toasted

In a heavy-based saucepan, gently sauté the onion, aubergine and garlic in the oil and butter for 5 minutes.

Stir in the rice and cook for 1 minute, then mix in the *garam masala* to taste. Add the carrot and stock, plus 1 teaspoon of salt. Bring to the boil, then cover pan and simmer gently for 15 minutes. Gradually stir in the spinach until wilted. Check the seasoning.

Serve sprinkled with cashews.

Brown Basmati and Red Bean Croquettes
Roz Denny

Crisp and tasty, these croquettes contain fragrant and nutty brown basmati rice bound with a purée of red kidney beans and cheese. Serve with a fresh tomato sauce and perhaps a nicely dressed green salad. Popular with children and adults alike. Make a batch and freeze what is left over.

Serves 8

255g/9oz/1¼ cups brown basmati rice
30g/1oz butter
1 tablespoon sunflower oil
1 small onion, chopped finely
1 small green pepper, chopped
2 cloves garlic, crushed
2 teaspoons ground paprika
1 teaspoon ground cumin
1 teaspoon ground coriander
1 teaspoon dried oregano
1 x 400g/14oz tin red kidney beans, drained
55g/2oz/½ cup mature Cheddar cheese, grated
55g/2oz/a cup cashew nuts or peanuts, chopped
2 eggs, beaten
Sea salt and freshly ground black pepper
Dried breadcrumbs, for coating
Vegetable oil, for deep frying

Cook the rice according to the packet instructions. Drain, season and cool.

In a large saucepan, heat the butter and oil. Gently fry the onion, pepper and garlic for 10 minutes, then stir in the spices and oregano and cook for another minute. Put the kidney beans into a food processor and beat to a rough purée.

Mix the rice with the vegetables, bean purée, cheese, nuts and 1 egg, and add salt and freshly ground black pepper. Chill until firm, then shape into 8 croquettes, dipping your hands in cold water if the mixture sticks.

Dip the croquettes into the remaining beaten egg, then coat well in the breadcrumbs. Heat the oil in a deep fat fryer to 180°C/350°F and fry for 3–4 minutes, until crisp and golden. Drain.

Serve with a chunky tomato sauce.

French Beans
Taze fasulye
Gönül Çilasun

Serves 4

750g/1lb 10oz French beans
2 cloves garlic, crushed
4 tablespoons olive oil
1 tablespoon brown sugar
Salt
1 teaspoon paprika
1 red pepper, chopped

Wash the beans and cut into 2.5cm/1 inch lengths. Fry the crushed garlic in the olive oil for a few minutes, then add the beans, sugar, salt, paprika and red pepper. Stir continuously for 5 minutes, then add 285ml/½ pint/1½ cups of boiling water and continue to cook gently until the beans are tender.

Serve hot or cold.

Green Beans in Tomato Sauce

Jane Whiter, Chef, Westminster Classic Tours

Serves 2–4

500g/1lb 2oz green beans or runner beans
Basic tomato sauce (see below)
Fresh flat-leaf parsley

Basic tomato sauce

1 medium onion, finely chopped
1 tablespoon olive or sunflower oil
1 large clove of garlic, finely chopped
500g/1lb 2oz plum tomatoes, peeled, or a 400g/14oz tin of plum tomatoes
1 tablespoon tomato purée
Salt and freshly ground black pepper
½ teaspoon sugar (optional)

Soften the onion in the oil over a medium heat, then add the garlic. After 5 minutes, add the roughly chopped tomatoes (if you are using tinned tomatoes, whiz them briefly in a food processor first). Add the sugar unless the tomatoes are very sweet, then leave to cook over a very low heat (perhaps using a heat diffuser) for about 30 minutes, checking from time to time, until you have a thick rich mixture.

Cook beans in sauce until soft.

TURKISH FAST FOOD

Turkish Fast Food

Osman Serim

Turkey has always had great street food. I don't know about Ankara, but in Izmir and Adana, and of course in Istanbul, the range is vast. Traditionally, though, it used to be considered ill-mannered for respectable Turkish families to eat in the street. As most Turkish towns are small, it is possible for people to go home for lunch, and where this is not possible, in the large cities, it has been customary to take food from home to work rather than eat out.

But what treasures these respectable families missed out on! Let us begin with the crusty pastries of Izmir. The first of these is known as the *simit*. This shares the same counter as *açma* and *çatal pogaça*, which are eaten in the morning still warm from the oven. Then there is ay *çöreği*, now sold only in patisseries; marzipan is the best known in this category. Let us next describe the savoury *böreks*. First there is the *kürt börek*, sliced and sprinkled with icing sugar, then there is the *sariyer börek*, with nuts, raisins and minced meat. There are also spinach and cheese *böreks* made with puff pastry. I haven't come across *su börek* in the street, but one finds *çig börek* being cooked to order by vendors, particularly in coastal resorts – in late afternoon, doughnuts will be made in the same oil. Warm doughnuts sprinkled with cinnamon are one of the unforgettable pleasures of a summer evening in Izmir.

Another popular choice is *lahmacun* (Turkish meat pizza). Usually vendors will carry it in baskets hanging from their arm, with other ingredients – lemon, parsley, finely sliced onion and red pepper flakes

– carried in a separate basket. Izmir's original *börek* of pitta with cheese is not so common now, nor is the warm sandwich made with the small *kumru* loaf. Lamb skull (*kelle*) from Izmir's Kemeraltı district, however, is another classic.

Then there is *tost*, the staple diet of the student. Kasar (cheese) is the cheapest topping. If you have the money there is double *kasar*, so thick that the melted cheese spills out and sticks to the wrapping paper. *Yengen* is another variant, made with tomatoes. These savouries are sold from small kiosks, or *büfes*. They are often eaten with Russian salad, a legacy from aristocrats who escaped the Revolution. This salad adopted its current name, 'the American', during the Cold War. Another popular Russian import, especially with the young, is *kumpir*, consisting of large potatoes cooked until soft, then filled with whatever comes to hand and eaten with a spoon.

In the Byzantine era, *kökoreç*, grilled liver in bread, seasoned with salt and pepper, was very popular; during the Ottoman period *arnavut* ciğeri (liver sandwich) was a great favourite, and liver continues to be an important street food.

On the Bosphorus, where fish is plentiful, filleted sardines are fried in oil, wrapped in bread, rolled in the previous day's newspaper and served to waiting customers. In this way it is possible to eat while reading yesterday's news at the same time. In recent years it has become a tradition to eat giant sandwiches filled with *sucuk* or *köfte* before a match. Likewise, before an evening's session, serious drinkers will buy stuffed mussels and *çig köfte* (an import from the southeast), made by street vendors while they wait. From the Aegean come chargrilled poussin or lamb *çöp şiş*, served on thin wooden skewers in a sandwich.

Let us look at some of the more varied and exotic street dishes. At the turn of the twentieth century, in the Pera district of Istanbul, barmen used to dispense fruit and alcohol punches from barrels carried on their backs. On special days, for example Bayram or perhaps the arrival of a funfair, huge numbers of street vendors would gather to sell their wares: *sekerli macunlar* and *keten* and *pamuk helva* sellers, *horaz* and *elma* confectioners; roasted and boiled corn-on-the-cob sellers, hawkers selling peeled and salted cucumbers, purveyors of *tulumba* and *tatlı simit*, traders in pistachios and other nuts, pumpkin and sunflower seeds; and, carrying large churns on their backs, the flavoured-syrup sellers, the *ayran* sellers, the mineral water sellers, the *köfte* sellers, and the *kökoreç* sellers. At such gatherings all these street traders would mingle and mix.

Of all street foods, perhaps the most famous and widespread around the world is the *döner*. The paper-thin grilled chicken, veal or lamb, served inside pitta bread with pickle, tomatoes and thinly sliced lettuce, is the sandwich preferred by those who want to eat cheaply.

I have in my mind a calendar of fruits. Spring conjures up green plums, almonds and strawberries, often sold outside schools. Summer brings melons, watermelons and peaches. Autumn suggests chestnut sellers. As for orange and mandarin, these recall the winter.

A strange vision has entered my head: it is past midnight, and half-drunk men congregate at bars and pavilions to purchase pilaf and chickpeas – perhaps because nowhere else is open, and, possibly to avoid their wives' scorn, they consume their takeaway on the hoof before arriving home.

As I write this I realize how much street sellers still hold a place in our lives. It reminds me of one of our journalist's articles in a Sunday paper. The journalist, after spending many years in New York, arrives back in Istanbul. He is awoken by an incomprehensible call coming from the street. When he looks over the balcony he sees a vendor pushing a cart. He asks the man, 'What are you selling?' The vendor replies, 'Governor, I am buying!' 'What are you buying?' the journalist asks. 'Governor, whatever it is, you sell it and I'll buy it!' The author was baffled and concluded his article: 'I've been to all of these places, seen all sorts of vendors, but a vendor buying!'

Börek

from Anton Mosimann's *Mosimann's World*

Pastry pies, large and small, are made all over the Balkans, the Middle East and North Africa. The pastry can be flaky or rough puff, *warkha* or filo, as here, and a bread dough is sometimes used. The *sanbusak* of Syria, Lebanon and Egypt are generally half-moon-shaped, the pasteles (*hamur işleri*) of Turkey are like little meat pies, and the brik of Tunisia are cigar-shaped. *Burekakia*, the filo pastries of Greece, are usually triangular.

Makes about 24–30

6–8 large sheets filo pastry
255g/9oz/2 cups crumbly white feta cheese
100g/3½oz/½ cup cooked spinach, finely chopped

1 teaspoon fresh oregano, chopped
1 tablespoon fresh parsley, finely chopped
1 nutmeg, freshly grated
Salt and freshly ground black pepper
55g/2oz butter, melted
1 egg yolk, mixed with 2 teaspoons water

Preheat the oven to 180°C/350°F/gas mark 4.

Unwrap the filo and lay the sheets on top of each other. Cut into 4cm/1½-inch-wide strips. Cover with a barely damp cloth while you make the filling.

Put the feta, spinach, oregano and parsley into a bowl and mix together to make the filling; it should be paste-like. Season to taste with nutmeg and freshly ground black pepper, but be careful with salt, as the feta will be salty already.

Brush one of the filo strips with melted butter, keeping the others under the damp cloth while you work. Place a spoonful of the cheese mixture on the top corner. Fold over into a triangle and then fold over again and again until you have reached the end of the pastry strip, resulting in a tight triangular package. Place on a baking sheet. Continue in the same way with the remaining filo strips, butter and filling.

Brush the tops of the little pastries with the egg wash and bake in the preheated oven for 10 to 12 minutes until puffed up and golden.

Serve hot.

Turkish Lamb Kebabs

Lesley Waters

Serves 4

455g/1lb boned leg of lamb, cut into 4cm/1½ inch pieces
Rind and juice of 1 large lemon
2 tablespoons olive oil
3 cloves garlic, peeled and gently smashed
Freshly ground black pepper
4 woody stems fresh rosemary
2 medium red onions, peeled, each cut into 8 wedges

Place the lamb pieces in a large bowl and add the lemon rind and juice, olive oil and garlic. Season generously with freshly ground black pepper. Pull the rosemary leaves from their stems and add to the lamb, reserving the stems. Mix well, cover and chill for 4 hours or overnight.

Take the pieces of lamb from the marinade and thread onto the rosemary stems, alternating with the onion wedges. Reserve the marinade.

Heat a griddle pan until hot. Add the kebabs and sear for 4 to 5 minutes on each side, basting frequently with the reserved marinade. Allow the lamb to rest for a couple of minutes.

Serve with chickpea and lemon salad.

Chickpea and Lemon Salad

Serves 4

1 x 400g/14oz tin chickpeas, drained and rinsed
1 medium mild salad onion
1 fresh red chilli, finely chopped
Juice and grated zest of 1 lemon
2 tablespoons extra virgin olive oil
1 bunch fresh flat-leaf parsley, roughly chopped
Freshly ground black pepper
Salt

Put all the salad ingredients into a large bowl and mix well. Season generously with freshly ground black pepper and a pinch of salt.

Turkish Meat Pizza
Lahmacun
Canan Maxton

I can best describe *lahmacun* as a pizza of Turkish origin. It is the ultimate street food in terms of its definitive taste, its ease of handling as a takeaway item to eat in the street and its value for money. In my childhood it used to be the food of the poorer sections of the community, but it has become very popular in recent years due to the increased interest in all types of street food. Its popularity has spread to fashionable restaurants, and it is easily made at home too.

It is best eaten rolled up, so the dough needs to be rolled out thinner than for pizza. *Lahmacun* should be fairly spicy, and goes well with a green or mixed salad.

Makes 12

For the base:
1 dessertspoon baking yeast
1 teaspoon sugar
115ml/4fl oz/½ cup warm water
500g/1lb 2oz/3 cups plain flour
2 medium eggs
1 tablespoon oil

For the topping

400g/14oz minced lamb
1 x 200g/7oz tin tomatoes
1 small bunch fresh parsley, finely chopped
1 onion, finely chopped
½ teaspoon *harissa*
1 teaspoon salt
Freshly ground black pepper
Chilli flakes

Add the yeast and sugar to the warm water, stir, and leave to rise for about 30 minutes.

Put the flour into a large mixing bowl and make a well in the middle. Add the eggs, the oil and the yeast mixture. Draw the flour into the middle of the bowl little by little while mixing all the liquid ingredients into it. The dough should be as soft as your earlobe. If too soft, add more flour, if too hard add a little more warm water. Knead the dough until well mixed, then cover the bowl with a damp tea towel and leave in a warm place, such as the airing cupboard, so that it can rise. The dough is sufficiently risen when it has doubled in volume, developed little holes on the surface and has begun to smell sour.

Roll into small balls, about the size of golf balls. Roll out thinly on a

floured board. Mix all the topping ingredients together and spread over each piece of dough.

Heat a non-stick frying pan and cook the underside of the *lahmacun* first. You don't need to add oil to the pan. Next put the *lahmacun* under a hot grill and cook the top – watch it continuously, as it must not be overcooked.

DESSERTS

Sweet Little History
Victoria Combe, *Daily Telegraph*

Turkish delight must be the only sweet in the world that is so embedded in a country's national identity. It was invented by Bekir Efendi, who came to Istanbul in 1777 from the eastern province of Anatolia. His first shop, Hacı Bekir, in a narrow street close to the spice bazaar, is still owned by his descendants and run by the fifth generation of the families he employed.

Bekir concocted the recipe for Turkish delight in 1777 as an improvement on an old mixture of honey or molasses, water and flour. He used cornflour and the newly available refined beet sugar and developed the firm, chewy jelly. Word spread, and the sultan appointed him chief confectioner to the palace. He travelled the world, winning medals in Vienna, Cologne, Brussels and Paris for the quality of his confectionery.

Little has changed in 226 years. The classic flavours remain: rose, lemon, mint and mastic. But the Turks' favourite – and the biggest seller – is a plain jelly studded with pistachios. Şeker Bayramı (the sweet festival), marking the end of Ramadan, is Hacı Bekir's peak season, when the company's four small shops can expect to sell 10 tonnes of Turkish delight in a day.

Turkish Delight
from Gary Rhodes's *Open Rhodes Around Britain*

Turkish delight has become an annual treat for me. Every Christmas a box of it seems to come my way and, I have to admit, I eat the lot!

Makes about 680g/1½lb

680g/1½lb/3½ cups caster sugar
285ml/½ pint/1½ cups water
55g/2oz/¼ cup glucose syrup
Approx 2 tablespoons rosewater
A few drops of red food colouring (optional)
110g/4oz/¾ cup cornflour
2 x 11g sachets powdered gelatine
30g/1oz/¼ cup icing sugar

Line a 20cm/8 inch square tin or mould (at least 2.5cm/1 inch deep) with cling-film.

Heat the caster sugar, water and glucose syrup with the rosewater and food colouring. Bring to the boil and cook for 8–10 minutes.

Add a drop of water to 75g/2½oz of cornflour to loosen. Soften the gelatine in water according to the instructions on the packet.

Remove the boiling syrup from the stove and add the gelatine. Once dissolved, whisk in the cornflour, cook for 2–3 minutes, then pour into the prepared tin or mould to about 2.5cm/1 inch deep. Allow to cool, then chill for 2–3 hours until completely set.

To finish, mix together the remaining cornflour and the icing sugar. Turn the gelatine mixture out of the mould and, using a warm wet knife, cut it into cubes. Roll them through the icing sugar and cornflour to coat lightly. Now all you have to do is eat it!

Kadayıf

Hüseyin Özer

Made with fine shreds of pastry resembling vermicelli, Turkish *kadayıf* is a dessert of great repute, and is known in Arab countries as *künefe*. The pastry encloses a fresh cream-cheese filling; and the whole thing is drenched in fragrant syrup and embellished with walnuts. Because the dough can now be bought from some supermarkets, as well as from Turkish grocers, the dessert is accessible to the home cook.

Serves 6

225g/8oz/1 cup caster sugar, plus 2 tablespoons
285ml/½ pint/1½ cups water
1 teaspoon rosewater
225g/8oz *kadayıf* dough
225g/8oz butter
300g/11oz/1⅓ cups Turkish Nor cheese, or ricotta, mashed
4–5 tablespoons walnuts, finely chopped

Put the sugar and water into a heavy-based saucepan. Stir over a gentle heat, and when the sugar has dissolved, stop stirring, raise the heat and bring the syrup to the boil. Let the syrup boil for 5 minutes, then stand the base of the pan in cold water to arrest cooking. When the syrup is cool, stir in the rosewater.

Spread out the *kadayıf* dough on a large flat dish or baking tin. Melt the butter and drizzle all but 3 tablespoons over the dough. With your fingers, work lightly to separate the strands of dough and moisten them with the butter. Continue until all the dough has turned from white to pale gold.

Arrange half the dough in an even layer in a non-stick frying pan about 25cm/10 inches in diameter. Add the cheese in an even layer. Spread the rest of the dough over the cheese and drizzle the remaining butter on top. Lightly flatten the whole thing, ideally with a smaller frying pan; otherwise use your hand. Cover with a lid.

Set the layered *kadayıf* over a low heat and cook for 20 to 25 minutes or until crisp and golden. During this time, turn it every 5 minutes, inverting it on to a plate then slipping it back into the frying pan.

Transfer the *kadayıf* to a large serving plate. Scatter with walnuts and ladle over the syrup, making a small pool around the edge of the pastry. Cut into portions, using a very sharp knife. *Kadayıf* is particularly good served hot, especially if you offer hazelnut or vanilla ice cream as an accompaniment. It is also excellent cold and keeps well.

Compote of Apricots, Prunes and Oranges
Kuru kayısı, kuru erik ve portakal kompostosu
Hüseyin Özer

Although this salad combines dried and fresh fruit, its flavours work harmoniously. It is extremely versatile, as suited to the breakfast table as to lunch or dinner. Make sure you remove all the pith from the oranges, cutting horizontally round each fruit to remove skin and pith together in a continuous spiral.

Serves 6–8

225g/8oz/1½ cups ready-to-eat dried apricots
225g/8oz/1½ cups ready-to-eat dried pitted prunes
455g/1lb/2¼ cups caster sugar
565ml/1 pint/2¼ cups water
1 large orange, free of peel and pith and sliced
2 tablespoons clear honey
30g/1oz/¼ cup walnut pieces

Put the dried fruit and sugar into a large saucepan. Pour over the water. Bring to a simmer, stirring gently to dissolve the sugar. Partially cover the pan and let the mixture simmer gently for 12 minutes, adding a little more water if the fruit ceases to be immersed in liquid. Add the slices of orange and stir in the honey. Simmer for a further 5 minutes.

Arrest the cooking by standing the base of the pan in cold water. When the compote is cold, transfer it to a serving bowl. Cover and chill for at least 1 hour. Add the walnuts just before serving, with yoghurt as an accompaniment.

Apricots with Cream, Almond & Pistachio

Kayısı tatlısı

Hüseyin Özer

A familiar feature of the Turkish dessert trolley is the display of these plump, orangey-toned apricots with what appears to be a green and white stripe running down one side. These *kayısı tatlısı* owe their stripe to whipped cream and chopped pistachios. Sometimes walnuts or almonds may replace the pistachios.

Serves 4

20 (about 170g/6oz/1 cup) dried apricots, soaked according to packet instructions
425ml/¾ pint/2 cups double cream
7 tablespoons icing sugar
About 7 tablespoons pistachios, finely chopped
20 whole almonds, blanched or toasted according to taste

Put the apricots in a saucepan with just enough water to cover, and simmer until plump and tender. This will take from 10 to 30 minutes, depending on the type of dried apricots. Drain, rinse under cold water, then drain again.

Whip the cream and icing sugar together to form firm, slightly grainy peaks. Spread out the pistachios on a plate. Take an apricot and pull the side seam gently apart to open up the fruit like a book. Place an almond in the middle, then use a knife to fill the centre of the apricot with cream. Almost close the apricot. The cream should ooze out along the seam – if it doesn't, add a little more. Dip the exposed line of cream into the pistachios. Repeat with the remaining apricots.

Transfer the apricots to a flat dish and serve within 3 hours. In the meantime, keep them in a cool place. Serve on their own or with Turkish coffee.

Easy Almond Cake

Bademli kek

Hüseyin Özer

You can put this cake together in next to no time, especially if you do the blending in a food processor. The cake keeps well, so it is worth making in a large quantity. It is also very versatile, good on its own, with yoghurt, with fruit or – most delicious – with a purée of dried apricots.

Serves 6–8

1–2 tablespoons melted butter
Flour for cake tin
170g/6oz unsalted butter, softened
200g/7oz/1 cup caster sugar
4 large eggs
140g/5oz/1¼ cups ground almonds
70g/2½oz/½ cup plain flour, sifted
¼ teaspoon almond flavouring
1–2 tablespoons sifted icing sugar

Prepare a 23cm/9-inch cake tin; brush with melted butter, then line the bottom with non-stick baking parchment. Brush the paper with melted butter and lightly coat with flour. Preheat the oven to 180°C/350°/gas mark 4.

In a large bowl, or in a food processor, beat the softened butter until smooth, then gradually beat in the sugar until light and fluffy. Beat in the eggs one at a time, then gradually beat in the ground almonds. When the mixture is well amalgamated, fold in the flour and stir in the almond flavouring. Transfer the mixture to the prepared tin and tap the tin on the work surface to ensure even distribution. Bake in the preheated oven for about 35 minutes, or until the cake is firm to the touch in the middle. Remove from the tin and cool on a wire rack.

Dredge the top of the cake with the sifted icing sugar. Alternatively, sift the sugar over 2cm/¾ inch wide strips of card, arranged in stripes or diamonds on the top of the cake – this will give the cake an attractive appearance when the strips are removed.

Baklava
Nadir Güllüoğlu

This is a very popular dessert in Turkey and the most famous internationally. First mentioned in 1473 in Fatih Sultan Mehmet's palace kitchen records, the five or six varieties listed increased to fifteen in the cookbooks of the eighteenth century.

The purity of the butter, the freshness of the filling, pistachio or walnut, honey or sugar, and the size and shape of the cooking tray are all of considerable importance, but rolling out the thinnest possible *yufka* dough is what really shows the degree of the chef's genius. (*Baklava* chefs seeking work with Turkey's richest houses were tested on the greatest number of their *yufka* layers through which the outline of an object could be discerned.) So says Nadir Güllüoğlu, chairman of the board of Karaköy Güllüoğlu, by the Bosphorus, where the golden, buttery, nutty-sweet *baklava* is made of forty *yufka* layers.

Almost all masters of *baklava* came from Gaziantep in southeastern Anatolia, including Mustafa Güllü, who brought his *baklava* skills to Istanbul in the mid-1800s. One of several international awards recently won by Karaköy Güllüoğlu was for *diabak*. This extra-light *baklava* can be enjoyed by diabetics and people on a diet, as it includes 33 per cent fewer calories, 53 per cent less cholesterol and 40 per cent less sodium but has the same taste.

It is a Turkish tradition to offer *baklava* on family anniversaries and other celebrations, including Ramadan, when it was ordered for Ottoman Empire soldiers; the citizens of Istanbul called the ceremony *Baklava Alayı* (baklava regiment).

Serves 15

255g/9oz butter, melted
1 x 450g/1lb pack filo pastry
500g/1lb 2oz/2 cups ground walnuts or pistachios
750g/1lb 10oz/3 cups granulated sugar
375ml/13fl oz/1½ cups water
1 teaspoon fresh lemon juice

Preheat the oven to 170°C/325°F/gas mark 3. Lightly brush a 22.5 x 32cm/9

x 13 inch baking pan with some of the melted butter. Lay the pastry sheets on a work surface and cover with a damp towel to avoid drying out.

Place one sheet of pastry in the pan, cutting it to fit, and brush with melted butter. Add a second pastry sheet and brush with butter. Repeat until you've used half the pastry. Spread the walnuts or pistachios over the pastry, then begin building more pastry sheets over the nuts, brushing with butter as before. Continue until all the sheets are used. Pour any remaining melted butter over the top.

With a sharp knife, cut through the pastry to create strips 5cm/2 inches wide, slicing diagonally across the pan so that the pieces will be diamond-shaped. (Squares can be cut if preferred.) Bake in the preheated oven for 1 hour, until pastry is crisp and golden brown.

Meanwhile mix the sugar and water together in a saucepan and bring to the boil, stirring frequently. Simmer for 20 minutes, then add the lemon juice. Remove from the heat and cover the pan to keep the syrup warm while the pastry finishes baking.

When the *baklava* is ready, drain the excess butter from the baking pan and brush the *baklava* with it, then slowly pour the syrup over the pastry. Leave to rest at room temperature for a few hours or overnight before serving.

Poor's Keshkül
Abdullah Korun

Hacı Abdullah, off Istiklal Caddesi in Beyoglu, is frequently cited by writers, chefs and customers who value food cooked in the traditional Ottoman style. Founded in 1888, the restaurant has followed the trade guild route of passing from father to son or from master to apprentice, to whose name it was then changed. The owner is now Abdullah Korun, and all of the restaurant's 700 dishes use the original recipes, though some of them only appear in ancient cookbooks which are sadly now out of print.

Your eyes as well as your nose help you to anticipate the good food you will enjoy at Hacı Abdullah. You are greeted by displays of fresh and bottled fruit and vegetables, trays of meat, *meze* and main dishes, with the tall-hatted chefs who cook them in attendance. The delicious aromas waft you through to the back room where you sit under the high, multicoloured glass-domed roof.

The original restaurant was called 'Abdullah Efendi'. It was a favourite of Sultan Abdülhamid II and many distinguished foreigners were brought to appreciate the sultan's chosen dishes. One of them, Poor's *keshkül*, was served in coconut shells when it came from Genoa.

Serves 4

675ml/24fl oz/3 cups milk
2 egg yolks
200g/7oz/1 cup sugar
125g/4½oz/¾ cup rice flour
1 teaspoon vanilla sugar
100g/3½oz/1 cup flaked almonds
40g/1½oz/½ cup dessicated coconut
Pistachios, very finely chopped

Beat the egg yolks into the milk. Add the sugar and allow to simmer gently over a low heat, stirring constantly. Put the rice flour into a bowl and add water, stirring until it thickens slightly. When the milk comes to the boil, add the rice flour mixture and stir.

Simmer for 2 or 3 minutes more, then add the coconut, vanilla and almonds and turn off the heat.

Pour into 4 individual bowls, sprinkle pistachios on top and serve cold.

Helva
Sevim Gökyıldız

It is a fact that wherever you live in Turkey, except in Istanbul and Ankara, where modern individualism has taken root, a day will arrive when a neighbour will knock on your door and offer you a dish of *helva*. This dessert, made from semolina (or flour), sugar, milk and butter, plays an important and enduring role in Turkish culture.

Helva, the 'taste of sweetness', assuages the pain of death and intensifies life's happiness. Where else is the 'taste of sweetness' so important? All the events of one's life become occasions for which *helva* is made and distributed: birth, circumcision, starting school, receiving a degree, completing military service and returning in good health, marriage, buying a house, setting out on pilgrimage to Mecca and returning as a *hajji*. During religious days and festivals *helva* is made and distributed to all the neighbours in the surrounding streets. I remember my maternal grandmother saying that *helva* must be distributed to every house that can smell it being made. Certainly every traditional Turkish home has a copper saucepan and a wooden spoon ready to make *helva*.

According to true believers, *helva* is a sacred food. The scent of its fried semolina will bring a sense of calm and wellbeing to the home, causing everyone blessed with its aroma to sigh in pleasure, 'What divine fragrance!' *Helva* has come to symbolize a spirit of togetherness, and the way it is made and the customs that surround its use serve to unite people. To make *helva* requires time and patience, so the laborious work of continuously folding the semolina over a low flame is shared together with neighbours, or, particularly after the death of a loved one, by all the relatives of the departed, who will take turns to stir the semolina in the saucepan.

Helva is served on small plates. Generally each neighbour receives the equivalent of one spoonful per head. It is important that the plate on which the *helva* is sent be returned full, some days later, as a reciprocating gesture of goodwill. The plate may be returned with another dish, or another dessert, or possibly with fruit picked from the garden. To return the plate empty would be considered disrespectful.

When we look at the kitchens of palaces we can see that *helva* was much liked by the sultans too. In the Topkapı Palace, for example, where meals were prepared for 4–5,000 people, one of the three grand kitchens, known as the *helvahane*, was dedicated to making *helva*, demonstrating the importance and the frequency of *helva*-making in the sultan's court. Fatih Sultan Mehmet loved a particular *helva* which became known as *hakan helva*s or the 'sultan's *helva*'.[1] Sultan's *helva* is one of fifteen varieties of *helva* described in the book The Chef's Quarters, dating from 1844, from whence the recipe for hakan *helva* is taken:

Identical quantities of pure flour, wheat starch and rice flour are mixed together in butter over a very low flame. Juice made of honey and milk is poured over, and the lid closed and the resulting *helva* simmered.

My maternal grandmother taught us to make the ideal *helva* in three easy steps: one measure of oil, two measures of flour and three measures of sugar. Modern dieticians condemn these ingredients as 'the three white enemies', and today's medical experts say that because of this *helva* should only be eaten in minute quantities. However, when we look at the desserts from the rest of the world we come across these three dangerous

---

1. Derived from the Ottoman Turkish *helya – i hakani* or 'Emperor's helva'

ingredients in great quantities. For example, to make *galettes bretonnes* (butter biscuits), for every 1kg/2lb 2oz of flour you must add 750g/1lb 10oz of butter and 750g/1lb 10oz of sugar. Even in the most basic tart pastry the quantities of flour and butter are the same as for *helva*. During times when sugar was scarce *helva* was made with honey or molasses, resulting in fewer calories but more taste and aroma. My opinion is that as long as one does not overindulge, *helva* is not dangerous to one's health.

Particularly during the fifteenth, sixteenth and seventeenth centuries, *helva* had another function in Turkish communities – the '*helva* sohbetleri', translated as '*helva* soirées'. People got together to play games, make conversation, listen to music and to eat. To round off the evening, *helva* was eaten to sweeten the mouth.

During the Ottoman Empire the *helva sohbetleri* were important gatherings that helped to maintain relationships within each social group. It is a pity that this fine tradition has failed to survive in our fast modern age, and that the tradition of *helva* distribution is endangered by more fashionable way of doing things.

Helva-making and distributing is still largely practised to commemorate death, but a house buyer, someone getting married or someone wishing to share their good fortune, rather than making *helva*, will buy a huge cake and share it with their friends. To follow in this lovely tradition is not difficult; instead of a cake, why not experience the pleasure of filling our house with the 'divine fragrance' and perhaps meet the person upstairs, downstairs or the neighbour next door whom we have never seen, to knock on their door and offer them *helva* on a plate?

Orchid Ice Cream

Eric Hansen, *Sunday Telegraph*

Researching his latest book, *Orchid Fever*, Eric Hansen headed for the Asian shore of the Bosphorus to contemplate what he thought were doubtful claims for orchid ice cream:

salepli dondurma – a pudding made from wild orchid tubers, milk and sugar that could, according to the experts, heal the spleen, prevent cholera and tuberculosis, facilitate childbirth, stop your hands and feet from shaking, and improve your sex life. *Salep* is a whitish-coloured

flour, milled from the dried tubers of certain wild, terrestrial orchids. Similar orchids grow throughout Europe, the eastern Mediterranean and Asia Minor, but the tubers used for this uniquely Turkish delicacy come from the mountainous edges of the Anatolian plateau.

According to Ali Kumbasar of Ali Usta in Moda, 'fox-testicle ice cream – the literal translation of *salepli dondurma* – originally came from Maraş (also known as Kahramanmaraş), a city in the southeast of Turkey, on the southern slopes of the Taurus Mountains, 300 years ago. Several species of orchids grow nearby, milk is available from cattle, sheep and goats, and snow is abundant for the freezing process. Similar orchid habitats exist elsewhere in Turkey but, for Turkish people, Maraş is the home of orchid ice cream.'

Eric Hansen adds: 'A hot drink, also called *salep*, is made from dried orchid tubers, sugar, milk and cinnamon. For hundreds of years it has been served during the cold winter months in Turkey and Greece, Syria, even Britain, where it is called *saloop*. Today, when Turkish men claim that the beverage is used for strengthening the body, it is abundantly clear which part of the body they are referring to.

Ali Kumbasar speculated that the first batch of *salepli dondurma* was probably a mistake – the result of a pot of hot *salep* freezing overnight. In an attempt to save his valuable ingredients, the *salep* vendor probably chipped and pried at the frozen ball of *salep* with a metal rod to extract the mixture from the pot. The stiffened mass of milk, sugar and *salep* turned out to be rather tasty, and this discovery led to further refinements. In time, the *salep* vendors developed the technique of kneading the mass of *dondurma* to a smooth consistency using hand-forged metal rods. The recipe for the taffy-like *dondurma* has changed slightly, but it is still necessary to eat it with a knife and fork.

Red and Yellow Melon Salad

Kavun karpuz salatası

Gönül Çilasun

Serves 6

1 melon
1 small sweet watermelon
285ml/½ pint/1½ cups orange juice
Juice of 2 lemons

140ml/¼ pint/just over ½ cup sour cherry liquor
4 fresh mint leaves

Cut each melon in half and scoop out the insides, keeping the skins of
the watermelon halves intact. Cut the melon flesh into small cubes. Mix
the orange and lemon juice, cherry liquor and mint and pour over the
fruit. Return the fruit to the watermelon skins.

Serve chilled.

Flaming Pears
Armut tatlısı
Gönül Çilasun

Serves 4

4 pears
1 glass white wine
½ wineglass granulated sugar
4 cloves
1 dessert spoon ground cinnamon
200g/7oz/1 cup caster sugar
1 wineglass brandy

Wash and peel the pears and place in a bowl. Bring the wine and granulated
sugar to the boil and add the cloves and cinnamon. Add the pears and
simmer until the fruit is cooked.

Transfer the pears to an ovenproof dish and cover with the caster
sugar. Pour the brandy over the pears and set it alight before serving.

Aegean Salad

Ege salatası

Gönül Çilasun

Serves 6

1 small melon
4 red apples
4 juicy pears
2 plums
1 wineglass sparkling wine
Juice of ½ lemon
Fresh cherries or decorative ones

Cut the melon, apples, pears and plums into small pieces. Mix the wine and lemon juice, pour over the fruit, and refrigerate. Decorate with the cherries.

Serve cold.

DRINKS

Raisin Sherbet

Kuru uzum serbeti

Canan Maxton

Sherbets are sweet, refreshing drinks. They usually have a fruit base to which water is added. They used to be served to guests on arrival, and can also be used during meals. Although most types of fruit can be turned into sherbet, I have chosen a very simple sherbet to acquaint you with this traditional drink. Serve it very cold or with ice.

Serves 6–8

500g/1lb 2oz/2½ cups raisins
1.5 litres/2¾ pints/6¾ cups still spring water

Wash the raisins, put them into a saucepan with the water, and cook on a medium heat until the raisins begin to melt. Leave to cool, then strain through a muslin bag and squeeze well to extract as much pulp and juice from the raisins as possible. Taste to make sure it is sweet enough. Add extra sugar, if desired.

Keep in the fridge for 24 hours before consuming. If you find the taste too strong, add more water.

Yoghurt Drink

Ayran

Canan Maxton

This is a traditional drink to be consumed on its own or as an accompaniment to a meal. It is a savoury drink, hence the addition of salt. To the uninitiated this might sound rather odd, as the usual way one encounters yoghurt in the West is in a sweet form. However, yoghurt is eaten with a lot of main meals and *meze* in Turkey and the Middle East. It is very refreshing when served with rice and meat dishes containing chilli.

Full-fat yoghurt makes a tastier *ayran*, but it is also good when made with low-fat yoghurt. In fact I prefer it.

Serves 6–8

500ml/18fl oz/2 cups yoghurt
1 litre/1¾ pints/4½ cups still spring water
Salt
½ teaspoon dried mint (optional)

Put the yoghurt and water into a large bottle with a stopper and shake until well mixed. Alternatively you could use a blender. Add the required amount of salt, depending on your taste. It should be fairly savoury without being too salty.

Add the mint and serve with ice.

Turkish Liquors

Sally Mustoe

Most Turkish Liquors have a real fruit flavour and are not too heavily alcoholic, so are ideal for use as marinades or to give an everyday recipe that Turkish touch.

Homemade pea and/or carrot soup can be improved by adding fresh roughly chopped coriander, poppy seed and *gül* (rose) liquor.

Create a deliciously different citrus taste with your goose or duck. Roast the bird on a rack over an oven tray to drain off the fat, as usual. Half an hour before it is ready, make cuts in the bird and rub in lemon pepper and *limon* (lemon) liquor.

Lemons for *limon likörü* (lemon liquor) are grown near Hatay, Adana, Rize and Trabzon and are harvested between December and February. Only the rind of the lemon is used. They are rich in aroma and in vitamin C, with vitamins A and B. Alcohol: 30°, sugar 196g per litre.

An ideal marinade for lamb chops or leg is *nane* (mint) liquor with cinnamon and fresh rosemary.

Slice bananas longways and place in an oven dish. Add *muz* (banana) liquor and cover. Leave overnight. In the morning, turn them over and cover again. When needed for lunch or dinner, sprinkle chopped nuts and grated dark chocolate over the bananas and cook in a moderate oven for 25 minutes. For a guest who prefers to have no alcohol, or for children, a separate dish using fruit juice is easy to substitute.

Muz likörü is made with bananas grown around Anamur, Antalya. Alcohol: 25°, sugar 216g per litre.

A quicker dish can be prepared using dried apricots. Pour over boiling water to cover. After about 15 minutes, when the water is absorbed, add a generous glass of *kayısı* (apricot) or *sheftali* (peach) liquor and cook in a moderate oven.

Apricots for *Kayısı likörü* come from Ayrancık near Konya. They also have a pleasant aroma and are rich in vitamins A, B and C. Alcohol: 27°, sugar 131g per litre.

Acıbadem's (bitter almond) nutty flavour makes it the perfect liquor for a fruit salad marinade.

Meze and Lion's Milk (Rakı)

Vefa Zat

When the English King Edward visited our country, Mustafa Kemal Atatürk invited him and Mrs Simpson (as an unofficial part of their visit to Istanbul) to the waterside château of Florya. Sir Percy Loraine, the British ambassador, also attended the banquet from Ankara. Also present was our great leader's school friend Ali Fuat Cebesoy.

Whiskies had been offered, the atmosphere was convivial and the conversation warm and sincere. During drinks King Edward said, 'I believe in Turkey the favoured drink is *rakı*; please do not hold back on my account, I would have drunk *rakı* too.' At this our great leader smiled and replied, 'This is quite so; however, my dear friend Ali Fuat Cebesoy and me, back in the days when we were at school, tried and liked whiskey and we're used to it.'

Rakı is indeed the favoured drink in Turkey. Over the years we have developed a tradition of *rakı*-drinking – an etiquette, if you will – and even now our interaction with others is still influenced by it. The etiquette of *rakı* requires painstaking effort with its accompanying setting, food and conversation, with its *meze*, its carafes, its glasses. *Rakı* is the drink to accompany special meals and conversations. Everything must be perfect.

In the past *rakı* was considered to be a 'mature man's' drink. It was considered unsuitable for women or youngsters, whom it was not usual to see in bars. If one did, one didn't think too highly of them, and it was out of the question to see a woman drinking *rakı* alone. If a woman was at a table with others, it would reflect badly on the whole company if she drank *rakı*, even if she was the wife of one of the men at the *rakı* drinkers' table.

For men the story was different – a proud father would celebrate the day that his son was old enough to join him at the *rakı* table. The boy had now become a man! He had come of age by drinking *rakı*.

But drinking *rakı* had its rules, and these rules had to be followed. These rules were established after debates in the community, and whenever the rules were changed, *rakı* was drunk. Despite our changing and developing trends in drinking, in our culture it is still only drunk according to etiquette. Following these customs, our bars are a bit bohemian, a bit like a traditional market booth, also a little tired and lifeless. It is, of course, natural to compare our modern-day bars with those of the Ottoman period. It seems from the records that there were similarities with our own drinking-houses and drinking etiquette, but since the nineteenth century the traditional drinking-houses have been changing.

What about the earlier drinking-houses, what kind of places were they? According to many sources the drinking houses in Constantinople harked back to the Byzantine period. Some of these sources mention that even at the time of Sultan Fatih Mehmet, Constantinople's drinking-houses were world-famous and exclusive to this great city.

During the Byzantine period the most widespread or perhaps the only alcoholic drink was wine. Sources say the Byzantines believed bread and

wine were the two nourishing elements. In some monasteries it is recorded that wine was even imbibed at breakfast. Monks had daily allowances of wine, and reducing this allowance was a form of punishment, as well as a necessary part of a monk's fasting regime. In Constantinople wine-making was only carried out in monasteries. The beautifully decorated rooms of the caravanserai used to be bustling and busy at all times of day.

It is recorded that in the palaces of Byzantium wine was the primary drink. Some of these wines were what we would today describe as vermouth – aromatic, and served with vegetables. In addition, fruits other than grapes were used – apricots, plums, dates and figs – and these were fermented and made into wine. When Ottoman soldiers marched into Istanbul the Byzantine soldiers opened drinking-houses to make themselves feel better. During the invasions Genovese boats continuously transported wine from the Greek islands to Istanbul. So Istanbul was famous for its drinking-houses, particularly in the Galata district, even in the Byzantine period.

During the Ottoman period Istanbul's consumption of alcohol was widespread, both among the general populace and in the palace, especially during the reign of certain sultans. In the early days wine was the most common drink; in fact the word *meyhane* means the place where wine is made sold and drunk, but since the nineteenth century *rakı* has become more popular.

Non-Muslim nationals were in the majority in Galata, Langa, Samatya, Kumkapı, Fener, Balat Cibali Hasköy and Kuzkuncuk. After the eighteenth century the large number of drinking-houses in Çengelköy, Arnavutköy, Yeniköy, Tarabya and Büyükdere were, as a rule, run by non-Muslims, particularly Greeks and Armenians. During the Ottoman period there were two kinds of drinking-house: the one licensed, the other operated illegally. Of the two, the licensed drinking-houses were the less numerous. In time a third type known as a 'standing' drinking-house was opened, and during the reign of Sultan Abdül Aziz a type of large wine shop came into existence. In addition, less reputable 'drunkards' drinking-houses or dens opened.

The licensed system flourished from the conquest of Istanbul until the beginning of the twentieth century, when it became obsolete. However, in recent years it has seen a revival with the approval of the authorities. These busy places have become the sole and unrivalled location for night-time entertainment.

The Ottoman Empire, under Fatih Sultan Mehmet, established religious toleration and freedom of conscience, creating respect for authority.

Non-Muslim minorities were able to drink alcohol and produce the liquor themselves. This tolerant attitude continued into the Republican period, when alcohol became completely legal. After the formation of the Republic, tradesmens' and fishermens' drinking-houses in coastal areas became popular. With the arrival of tavernas and luxury live music restaurants, the traditional drinking-houses have sadly, one by one, been consigned to history.

'Den-style' *balozlar* existed until the beginning of the twentieth century, and during the Republican period 'standing' drinking-houses flourished briefly. This was also the period when the Ottoman Turks gradually began to operate drinking-houses. It was also during this time that one of the special ingredients that form the character of *rakı* was first used – dried grape flakes. The primary reason for using dried grape flakes was to do with the phylloxera disease that had threatened vintners since 1371.

The pulp left over from wine fermentation was mixed with spirit and aniseed and used in making *rakı*. This process lasted until the First World War when, because of shortages, not only dried grapes but also figs and even mulberries were used. The dried grapes are first sliced, then mixed with water and cultured; the resulting wine is distilled, and dried grapes are the result. After some time these dried grapes were put into traditional copper churns and mixed with aniseed. In this respect it was very similar in quality and character to the *rakı* of today. In slang *rakı* is known as *akyazılı*, *gıravatlı*, *anzorot*, *apeki*, *carmak*, *carmakcur*, *dem*, *duziko*, *duz*, *islim*, *istim*, *pirne*, *piyiz*, *piriz* and *süt*. Of its many aliases the most widely used is 'lion's milk'. There is even a type of *rakı* produced in Germany today with this name. They say that the term derives from the decorative lions that were embossed on the traditional urns in which the *rakı* was stored. Perhaps it has something to do with the way that clear *rakı* turns milky white when water is added.

Rakı is said to give you the courage and strength of a lion. It is true that it gives one the same Dutch courage as any alcoholic drink, but that is all! It doesn't have any magic properties.

'*Çilingir* Banquet' is the name given to our *rakı* meals, where *meze* are served on small dishes. *Meze* means 'taste' or 'tasty' and derives from the Persian. In the palace, to make sure that the sultan's food was not interfered with, a chief taster would consume small portions, and these small dishes have somehow found their way into ordinary people's kitchens. It is rumoured that the term *çilingir* (*hors d'oeuvres*) originated from the word *çeşnici* (food taster).

Let us now open the doors of our drinking-houses and find out what goes on in these places.

The licensed drinking-houses were run by a manager known as a *barba*, literally translated from the Italian for 'bearded old man'. While these managers were tolerant and naturally bohemian in their outlook, they didn't hesitate to display authority when occasion demanded. Food and drink was served by a *saki*, young boys called *micos* would help the manager, and an assistant known as a *mastori* would look after the distribution counter. A chef would prepare the food, aided by an assistant called a *yamak* ('mate').

In the licensed drinking-houses the young boy who brought the candlesticks and lit them at the customers' tables was called ateşçi (fire-lighter). The boys were aged between ten and fifteen and were also known by a Greek term, *pedimu* (my little one). In addition to the serving staff, particularly in the licensed drinking-houses, there were male dancers to cheer up the guests, known as *köçek* or *tavşanoğlan*.

Before the drinking-house opened its doors, the *saki*s and the *ateşçi* boys would change into fresh clothes and comb their fringes before putting on their fezzes. Their sleeves and hems rolled, clogs on their feet, cummerbunds around their waists, their shirts white as snow, and with braided waistcoats, they would stand ready to serve the regular customers. After the candles were placed in their holders the *saki*, with a flower behind his ear, would greet the guests, saying, 'Welcome, welcome,' greeting those he knew by name. The table would be set; the *barba* would personally put the candles on the table and would greet the guests by saying, 'Gentlemen, welcome.' After this the 'fire-lighter' would light the candles and would also greet the guests with 'Gentlemen, welcome.'

Every drinking-house had a central oil lamp, the lighting of which signalled the beginning of a jovial evening. The manager would ring a small bell at closing time, at which those who had been asleep or unconscious would awake, and, one by one, leave and enter the dark streets outside.

During the Republican era bars, tavernas and modern restaurants overtook the traditional drinking-houses. During the 50s and 60s many *barbas* such as Toma (from Gaskonyali), Mösyö Dimo (Dimitro), Kör Agop, Camur Şevket, Serkis, Minas, Ancelo, Todori, Anastas and Antranik Baronyan were responsible for preparing numerous sumptuous *meze* in their establishments, and at least made sure all experienced something of the traditions and customs of the drinking-house. Today only a small number of drinking-houses exist. The ones that come to mind are: Sefa (in Yedikule); Kuledibi, Gülendem, Huzur and Antik (Samatya); Kor

Agop, Minas, Olimpiyat, Sahil, Merkez, Iskele, Evren, Devrez, Bohem, Carretta (in Kumkapi); Aleko (in Yenikoy); Hristo (in Tarabya); Refik and YakupIn (in Asmali mescit); Agora (in Balat); Hisar (in Tarlabaşi); Despina (in Tepebaşi); Sadrazam (in Sütlüce); Koço (in Moda); Candaş (in Pangaltı); Ogun (in Yeşilköy); Cumhuriyet (in Balık pazarı); and Pasajı and Nevizade, Boncuk and Imraz (in Çiçek) .

And what are the traditional drinking-house *meze* and snacks? Well, here is a selection:

- Salted tuna brains garnished with sweet red onion
- Salad of fennel and sun-dried mackerel softened in vinegar
- Hay-smoked mullet
- Anchovies
- Fish paste with anchovies, or sometimes sprat in an oil dressing
- Fried mussels with hazelnut sauce, or mussel salad
- Stuffed mussels and mussels in bean salad with oil and onions
- Scallops, oysters, prawns, crab, Japanese red fish roe
- Black Russian caviar
- Cooked prawns
- Cooked lobster
- Octopus salad
- Fried squid
- Grilled bluefish
- Fried turbot
- Swordfish kebabs with bay leaves
- Steamed red gurnard and stuffed mackerel
- Intestines, hazelnuts and sweetbreads
- Grilled shepherd's garlic salami
- Dried and spiced fillet of dried meat
- Stuffed large-intestine sausage
- Tripe and vegetable stew, made with potatoes, onions and chickpeas
- Vine leaves stuffed with rice, red bean salad, artichokes in olive oil
- White bean salad with thinly sliced boiled egg decorating the top
- Fried aubergine with tomato sauce
- Circassian chicken with walnuts
- Albanian liver garnished with white bean salad with onions
- Taramasalata
- Boiled tripe, mashed broad beans, natural yoghurt with grated cucumber and garlic

- A variety of salads, slices of toasted French bread, butter, thyme and lemon juice
- Soaked black pressed olives, feta cheese, and Gruyère cheese
- Peeled fresh almonds on a bed of ice
- Fresh walnuts
- *Istragalya* (white chickpeas, salted then toasted over a brazier with the skins on)
- All types of fruit, the first being scented oval yellow melon

The custom is to start with a double measure of *rakı*, a portion of feta cheese and a slice of melon and then, depending on one's financial situation, black caviar and lobster salad. In short, as every *rakı* connoisseur will know, *rakı* should always be served with *hors d'oeuvre* style food, and the measure must be a double.

May your *rakı* be like cream, your table abundant and your conversation overflowing!

Turkish Wines

Sally Mustoe

Does it matter if library and Internet sources, professional wine writers and amateur enthusiasts disagree about whether wine-making in Turkey started 3,000 or 6,000 years ago? They do agree that Turkey is almost certainly the very place where man first tasted wine.

Hittites and Persians, Greeks, Romans and early Christians practised viticulture while in Turkey. Ali Esad Göksel writes:

A large stone relief found at Ivriz near Ereğli in the province of Konya depicts the Hittite god of wisdom and fertility, Tarbu, holding a vine branch with bunches of grapes in his right hand and ears of wheat in his left. The small human figure facing the god is the Hittite king Varpalavas, whose two hands are joined in supplication. The god Tarbu is giving Varpalavas the most precious foods he has: grapes and wheat. The Phoenicians, a seafaring people living on the shores of Anatolia, became rich selling wine to the Aegean islands and mainland Greece.

The historic vineyards of the Euphrates valley are still cultivated. Hugh

Johnson, in *The World Atlas of Wine*, cites Turkey as 'the most important grape-grower of the Levant with the fifth largest vineyard acreage in the world'. The Ottoman Empire exported nearly 70 million litres in one year in the 1890s, when only Christians and Jews made the wine. Kemal Atatürk, founder of the secular republic, built state wineries in the 1920s, but wine is still less popular nationally than the aniseed-flavoured *rakı*. The state monopoly accounts for most exports. Today, 80 per cent of the 300 million litres produced by nearly fifty wineries is exported. Doluca and Kavaklıdere are the leaders in this field.

About 40 per cent of all Turkish wine comes from Thrace and Marmara; for instance, the Doluca wineries are around Mürefte, a coastal town whose ancient name means 'a thousand flowers'. Their most modern winery, with vineyards on the Gallipoli Peninsula, is the first Turkish producer to concentrate exclusively on using the best-known international varieties of grapes.

A further 40 per cent is produced in Anatolia, much of it by Kavaklıdere, near where Noah came to ground after the Flood. In the area around Cappadocia, where the richly mineralized volcanic soil has been cultivated by grape-growers for thousands of years, the dramatic 'fairy chimneys' landscape yields a million tonnes of grapes a year, making 12.5 million litres of wine, as well as table grapes, currants, vinegar and *pekmez* (grape juice molasses). Until a generation ago, wine-making would have taken place in every home; older inhabitants of the Cappadocia valley still tread their own grapes by foot. At nearby Üchisar, Kocabay has also been producing table wines for more than thirty years, using their own and imported grapes, ageing them in huge tanks cut into the rock beneath their factory. According to Adnan Karaoğlu, 'The production of the Cappadocian table variety as well as fine wines is necessary. Cheap wine will always find a market, the drinking of fine wines is an art only recently rediscovered by Turks.'

The remaining 20 per cent of Turkish wine comes from the Aegean coast around Izmir.

The choice of a Turkish wine is, as with those of other origins, dependent on the food it accompanies, although many people find a glass or two enjoyable at any time. Again, we find our experts put forward a varied range of personal preferences but most recommended Yakut from Kavaklıdere, the Dolucas and Buzbağ, which is described as 'a wine of powerful yet pleasing character'.

Turkey is a secular republic, though Islam is the religion of almost all Turks. In the seventeenth century, in spite of the pleasure he is known to have taken in wine, Sultan Murad IV forbade his subjects to drink wine or smoke tobacco. Wine-drinking was prohibited, but the eulogies to wine written by the enormously popular mystic poets Mevlana and Omar Khayyam were widely appreciated. Ali Esad Göksel quotes Dr Altay Yavuzeser:

> The Ancient Turks presented wine to their sky god and believed that evil spirits kept away from places where there were vineyards and wine. When a child was born, it was customary to bury a jar of wine to be opened on its wedding day.

Perhaps the last word should go to Kemal Atatürk, as it does so often. He promoted Turkey's wine trade but advised 'moderation in all things'.

Turkey: A Land Flowing with Pure Spring Water
Belma Ötüş-Baskett

As Turkish cuisine emerged over the centuries as one of the most distinctive in the world, so too did a unique approach to the provision of drinking water. Doubtless through uncounted generations, and through trial and error, this method was shaped by necessity and availability.

All societies understand the basic necessity of pure drinking water, especially as urbanisation has progressed. In Turkey, however, more so than in many areas of the world, there was a source of safe water close at hand, if only it could be tapped: the underground springs in most areas of the country, not least in the capital, Istanbul. From an early date, the greatest act of charity a public figure or wealthy individual could perform was to build a fountain – *çeşme* – above a spring, thus providing drinkable water for the poor of the area, who otherwise would have been forced to take their chances with whatever water they could find.

In time, a special culture grew up around individual springs, each believed to possess special health-promoting properties. This was strikingly true of the many springs located among the hills of Istanbul, whose particular benefits residents identified and handed down through the generations. Thus today, as in the past, it is the custom for many people

to vary the spring water they consume according to the season of the year. In winter, 'heavy' waters, rich in minerals, are drunk to facilitate the digestion of rich dishes eaten in cold weather. In spring the blood needs to be 'thinned', so 'light' waters are preferred. In summer, water used to be kept in earthen jugs that 'sweated', thus keeping it cool. And in autumn, the water was changed in accordance with the diet of the season.

A partial list of the best spring waters in the Istanbul area includes Sırmakeş, Çırçir, Karakulak and Kayış Dağı. One of the most benevolent acts of Sultan Abdul Hamid in the late nineteenth century was to build fountains throughout Istanbul, with pure spring water flowing from the pipes. These fountains are called *Hamidiye*, after the Sultan. It is excellent drinking water, and one can still see people with jugs and bottles queuing to fill them up with the special *Hamidiye* water. Fountains were built by many benefactors and could be as architecturally elaborate as was desired. Many people know the beautiful Sultan Ahmet III fountain outside the gates of Topkapı Palace, which is a veritable monument to the life and times of its benefactor. Often the fountains have clever little poems that in Ebcet code (a system of transposing numbers into words) hide the date the fountain was built and end in a supplication to the drinker to remember the builder of the fountain in prayer. Thus these fountains can also be seen as repositories of Turkish culture.

There are also springs with foul-tasting 'curative' waters that are thought to be effective in treating various ailments of the liver, gall bladder, urinary system, etc. Tuzla, just outside Istanbul on the Marmara Sea, according to connoisseurs, has had a well-deserved reputation for centuries. Such places are usually called *içmeler*, and people go there to take the cure for a day or for a week, just as they do at the spas in the Black Forest. Turks in Germany often visit these spas because the older Turks still remember how the ailments of their elders were cured by 'the waters'.

Not all the benefits of spring waters are confined to the cities. On the outskirts of towns in Anatolia, picnic areas are often built around a fountain, or even an open spring. Driving along the highways, if you see vehicles stopped in an area it is likely that there is ice-cold water gushing up from a deep spring in the vicinity. There are many springs in the mountainous areas of Turkey, and there are many well-known brands of water bottled from these sources and shipped all over Turkey. The first ever was Afyon Karahisar Maden Suyu, made available through the efforts of the Turkish Red Crescent – a benevolent deed as well as one that has provided income to the Red Crescent for decades.

The natural volcanic 'sparkling water' that is abundant in Turkey also became available to the public at large. The extent of natural springs in Turkey was recently discovered by highway engineers tunnelling under the Bolu mountain to complete the divided highway connecting Istanbul and Ankara. There was so much water that the project had to be abandoned.

One of the great delights of driving over the winding mountain roads of Anatolia in summer is to come upon a roadside spring. Just such an experience can be had when driving south from Konya over the Taurus mountains to the Mediterranean. A few hundred feet from the Sertavul Pass (1,630 metres) a simple spring seems ideally placed to give one's journey a special, salubrious dimension.

Turkish Coffee
from Kurukahveci Mehmet Efendi

Among the Turks, coffee and the way it is served play a very important role in establishing and strengthening the bonds of friendship and, in every Turkish house, offering Turkish coffee is still an important ceremony. In Turkish tradition, to accept a cup of coffee is to do honour to the one offering it; the Turkish saying 'I'd drink his coffee' is taken as an expression of respect. Coffee once shared has implications that outlive the coffee itself: it suggests peace, friendship, love and respect. This sentiment is crystallized in the Turkish expression: 'The memory of a single cup of coffee lasts forty years.'

Because of its stimulant properties, Turkish coffee is frequently offered as a pick-me-up when one shows evidence of being tired. The coffee flavour that is left in the mouth lasts longer than other coffees. Even if drunk frequently, the quantity ingested each time is small enough to prevent a bloated feeling and the caffeine intake is moderate. Turkish coffee is made only from high-quality Arabica beans. In 1871, Kurukahveci Mehmet Efendi was the first person in Turkey to commercially roast coffee beans, then sell to the public. The family business is still flourishing.

A kind of fortune-telling is born out of Turkish coffee. The coffee grounds left in a cup are shaken a little by the person whose fortune is to be told, then the cup is covered with a saucer and turned over. (Some

people make a wish by touching the bottom of the cup with their index finger.) Once the cup has cooled, the fortune-teller usually starts by saying, 'Whatever is your state, so be your fortune told,' and tries to interpret intuitively the coffee-ground shapes in the cup. They must be solely good wishes; for instance, a palm tree indicates a holiday with new places and new people. A shape like the sun's rays symbolizes that your wildest dreams will suddenly be realized.

Coffee seems to have been originally introduced into the Ottoman Empire in the early sixteenth century when Özdemir Pasha, a governor of Yemen during the reign of Süleyman the Magnificent (1520–66), authorized its use in his own household and in the palace. In 1615, merchants from Venice were entranced by this flavour. In 1650, the first coffee was exported to Marseilles. In 1669 Turkish coffee was introduced to the society of Paris at the coffee parties arranged by the Ottoman ambassador, Süleyman Ağa. Coffee also reached Vienna in 1683, just after the city had been besieged in war with the Turks.

The culture of coffee and coffee shops has spread from Turkey to all over the world. The roots of coffee culture throughout the world today can be traced back to Turkey.

Making Turkish Coffee in Two Minutes

Mehmet Efendi's finely ground Turkish coffee should be prepared in a *cezve*, a small metal jug with a handle about 10cm/4 inches long.

For each serving: pour 1 demitasse full of fresh water (65ml/2½fl oz/⅓ cup) into the pot and add 1 heaped teaspoon of coffee, with sugar to taste. Stir the mixture thoroughly over a low heat.

When the coffee froths up, pour a little of the foam into each cup. Return the *cezve* to the heat, and as soon as the coffee froths up again pour it into the cups.

Never stir the coffee once poured into the cup, and be sure to sip it gently so as not to disturb the grounds. Turkish coffee is always served with a glass of fresh water.

Cheese

by Semih Sömer

Cheese is known and eaten lovingly almost everywhere in the world. It is hundreds and thousands of varying delights, according to the country. It forms part of cultures, and pride is taken in it. There exist many articles and books about it, as the adage in Turkey's culture of food and drink has it, '*Peynir, ekmek, hazır yemek*' ('Bread and cheese are fast food'). That is to say, cheese is something that is eaten with bread at any time.

It is a food with characteristics that differ within a region and even between villages very close to each other. Cheese is inevitably to be found wherever cattle are reared and milk is available. Milk in its natural state sours very quickly, and the more possibilities increase and cattle-rearing develops, the more the quantity of the product grows. In Turkey, cheese is made from the milk of cows, sheep, water-buffalo and goats. But traditional Turkish cheese is made from creamy sheep's milk in April and May. The milk of beasts that have grazed in meadows has the richest aroma.

What is consumed in the country at large, for the most part in the big cities, is *beyaz peynir*, a white cheese kept in tins and ripened in cold storage. The most highly regarded are known by the names Edirne, Ezine and Bigadiç; made from full-cream sheep's milk with the traditional fermentation, it is ripened for at least 6 months. This kind of cheese is made not only in the Marmara region but also around Antalya, Muğla and Burdur. In taverns and licensed restaurants it is the most popular accompaniment to *rakı*. It is also served traditionally at breakfast, with olives and tea.

The other much-consumed cheese is *kasher* (*kaşer*). The traditional *kasher* is made from full-cream sheep's milk and kept in cold-rooms for at least 6 months. Nowadays there are varieties made from cow's milk or a mixture of cow's and sheep's milk. The Kars region and Edirne are famous for *kasher*. In recent years this cheese has begun to be made on an industrial scale, where taste is less important; this is used for toasted sandwiches and pizza.

Interestingly, skin cheese (*tulum peyniri*), made in districts within an area ranging from northeast to southwest, is also gradually gaining esteem commercially and is increasingly used in kebab shops. This cheese, the original form of which is made in animal skins and kept for a long time in cool caverns and hollows, has recently begun to be stored in plastic containers.

Cheeses made in rural areas of Turkey are generally kept in brine and are designated by districts – Bursa, Antep, and so on. They can be found in local markets. To this class of fresh cheese we may add lor (goat's milk curd cheese). Used in the making of *börek*, which occupy an important place in Turkish food culture, lor is made from whey. It is generally fat-free, but the fatty lor made from the whey of Mihaliç cheese in the Balikesir region has a very special taste. Mihaliç cheese is hard and, because it stays for a long time in brine, is salty. Herb cheese, made at Van using various herbs (the one most commonly used is *sirmo*), finds customers in big cities outside the region. Çökelek, found all over Anatolia under various names and of varying quality, is categorized as lor.

Yoghurt is very important to Turks. Its fermentation and the system of making it are along the same lines as cheese. The fact that these products, when dried, are edible over long periods reflects Turkish culture in the full sense from the historical point of view. Dried milk is much used in areas of Central Asia that have a Turkish heritage, as much as in Anatolia. These long-lasting and dried derivatives of cheese are used as flavouring in soups and pasties.

Herbs & Spices

by Canan Maxton

Herbs and spices have played an important role in Turkish cuisine for centuries. Herbs are used not only in fresh form in salads and *meze*-type dishes but also as major ingredients in cooking.

Taste is not the sole asset for which herbs are valued. Claims are made for specific uses in physical and mental well-being; for instance, tarragon eases stress, thyme has antiseptic properties, parsley is extremely rich in vitamin C, fennel aids the digestion and sage is renowned for prolonging an active life. However, Turkish cuisine uses herbs mainly for their culinary properties.

When I was a child I was regularly sent out to the little stand at the corner of our street to buy what my mother referred to generically as *salata*, without specifying its constituent parts. I would repeat the same word to the *salatacı* – the salad vendor – and would return home with the following: 2 heads of lettuce, a bunch of spring onions, a bunch of radishes, a bunch of parsley and a bunch of dill. In spring, bunches of rocket and fresh garlic – which resembles chives or the green parts of spring onions – were added to this list, depending on availability. It never would have occurred to me, or to the salad vendor, to think that a household might not actually need this much parsley or dill every day. But we did get through it. Ways of shopping have changed dramatically over the years, but the Turkish household still uses a large amount of herbs, both fresh and dried.

The uses and varieties of herbs vary considerably from area to area in the country. Parsley, dill, thyme, mint and oregano are the most popular herbs in all regions of Turkey. The Aegean area is famous for

its green herbs – lamb's lettuce, sorrel, coriander, tarragon and many forms and colours of basil. However, in Istanbul these particular Aegean herbs, before the spread of fancy supermarkets offering foods from all corners of the world, were to be found only in specialist shops in and around the spice bazaar – Mısır Çarşisi – and attracted mainly Iranian, Azerbaijani and Arab consumers. Some fifty years ago, most inhabitants of Istanbul would never come across fresh coriander or basil, unless they had connections with the Aegean area or with minority groups.

The southeastern part of Turkey is where the hottest food is eaten. Hot chillies, fenugreek, fennel, dried ginger, nutmeg, cumin, cinnamon, onion seeds, coriander and cardamom seeds play a significant role in the local delicacies. Pungent spices seem to be the trademark of the cuisine of the area. *Çiğ köfte*, raw meatballs, a speciality of the region, could hardly be imagined without the addition of hot chillies. In fact, it is said that the hot chillies 'cook' the raw meat during the fairly long kneading and preparation of the mixture.

A variation on the herb and spice theme is the use of rosewater and orange-blossom water in sweets and desserts. These impart a particularly Ottoman flavour and an elegant aftertaste to the last morsels of a meal.

Olive Oil

by Tuğrul Şavkay

It is perhaps not widely known that Turkey is one of the world's great producers of olives and olive oil. After Spain (annual olive oil production 1.5 million tonnes), Italy (500,000 tonnes) and Greece (300,000 tonnes), Turkey's annual production of 250,000 tonnes competes with Tunisia for fourth place.

Turkey's production of olives varies between 1.2 million tonnes in a non-fallow year and 300,000 in a fallow year. On a 33 per cent correlation between the olive and its oil, this results in an annual yield of 400,000 and 100,000 tonnes of olive oil, or an average of 250,000 tonnes.

At this stage we should perhaps explain the significance of 'fallow' and 'non-fallow' to those not familiar with the world of olives. These terms refer to the fact that while an olive tree will give generously one year, the next year it will give less, due to a variety of factors that include farming conditions, husbandry techniques and fertilization methods. In Turkey the differences can be dramatic, so that in a non-fallow year each tree may produce 20 to 25 kilos, while in a fallow year it falls to just 6 kilos.

Although productivity is important, it is only one factor for the successful producer of olive oil. Quality is also vital, and here Turkey is very fortunate, for her natural terrain has enabled her to produce oils of superior quality. However, to produce good olive oil and to market it is not the same thing – as the Turks are now discovering. The Turkish olive oil trade is complex – one would have to be an olive oil *dégustateur*, or an expert in the world of John le Carré, to understand everything that goes on, the branding and marketing of the product is so poor. We owe the relative weakness of the olive oil trade to the failure of Turkish politicians, who, until the 1980s, did not treat the market as seriously as they should and have therefore failed to market the produce or learn from overseas experience.

Complaints aside, when we come to Turkish olive oil we find little has changed over the centuries, and to differentiate between the good and bad is still an interesting challenge. Rome was not built in a day, but let us try to identify the qualities that distinguish a good olive oil.

The best olives for pressing come from the Gulf of Edremit, known as 'the Gulf', which stretches between the Straits of the Dardanelles in the north to the Burhaniye region in the south. The Gulf lies between the Kaz Daglari, or Goose Mountains, to the east and the Aegean to the west. This region provides both meadow and hillside conditions, good sunshine as well as cold winters that produce a particularly good fruit. The Gulf of Edremit produces rich aromatic olives, particularly if harvesting is early, and the superior aroma is accompanied by finer taste. In the better examples it is often possible to feel a pleasurable hot sensation at the back of the throat.

While we are proud of Edremit's virtues, we should not imagine that this is Turkey's only olive oil. Further south, in the Aegean, the Memecik olive actually accounts for 75 per cent of all Turkish olive production. While this olive is eaten, 26 per cent of the crop is reserved for pressing. I personally find its oil rather heavy and its aroma unexceptional. As for Memecik, so for Memeli from the smaller lower region of Menemen.

There is another type of olive, peculiar to the Aegean, the *eşek* or 'donkey' – its name presumably deriving from its large plump shape. Because of its large size we only get between 80 and 100 olives to the kilo. Its appearance is similar to the Greek *kalamata*, and reminds one of this type when pickled in brine. In recent times, in polite circles, there has been a campaign to change the name to *çelebu/çelebi*. This olive has not been tested for production of olive oil. Nor has there ever been a great demand for it on tables for daily use. It produces a 'round' taste when first pressed, with a 'green' aroma.

Uslu, from Akhisar-Manisa, is another important Turkish olive. While it has not been tested for its olive oil production, it is pressed for local consumption and what remains is used for everyday use at the table.

Another undeservedly neglected olive is the *domat* of Akisar. As well as being a remarkable fruit, this olive produces marvellous oil, the colour of tomatoes (*domates*), from whence it derives its name. In its dried pressed state, when its oil is dripping, there are not words enough in the dictionary to describe its heavenly aroma. This olive has not been pressed for its oil before because its fruit is most abundant only after it has lost its best aroma.

As someone born and bred in the south of the Aegean it took me quite a while to get used to the thin and delicate oils of the north. There are many reasons for the differences in flavour – soil conditions, time of harvesting, and sometimes exceptional microclimates produce very interesting local oils such as those of the Milas area. Similarly, outside the Aegean and Marmara districts, the Antep region has gained a reputation as an olive oil producer. Nizip oil, from the olive-producing region of the same name, is thicker than Aegean oil and does not have the same delicacy. The same goes for the smaller lower region of Antalya.

Almost all of Turkey's oils that are produced for the industry come from the Gulf. For the more interesting oils you need to search locally, because these do not reach the normal markets. For these oils production is done according to ancient processes. Sometimes this is a stone mill dating from Roman times, or an ancient hydraulic press from a later period; or, from an even earlier period, a wooden barrel lined with sacking, filled with the oil and pressed with the foot. You will not come across any of these methods anywhere else in the world. As for the oils themselves, they are as interesting as the methods by which they are produced.

Aegean Cuisine

by Ahmet Örs

The cuisine of a region reflects the economic and cultural riches it has witnessed throughout history. However rich the life lived by the inhabitants of those lands in ages past, the culinary legacy they will bequeath to subsequent generations, like the cultural treasures, will be no less rich.

A fine example of this is the western portion of Turkey, the Aegean region. Nowadays this part of the country has an immensely rich food culture. In the history of civilization, people of many nations have lived in these lands, ranging from the Phoenicians to the ancient Egyptians, Athenians, Macedonians, Romans, Byzantines, Ottomans, Venetians, Christian knights and Arabs. Some lived there for long periods, some came for trade or in transit. But among the latter were some who settled down and stayed. They all lived in prosperity and comfort, at the same time contributing their traditions and customs. The result was an exceptionally rich treasury of culture.

Consequently, when we look at Aegean food, we find a flawless synthesis of cuisines. Throughout the ancient Greek and Roman eras, the Aegean coasts of Anatolia provided Europe with the olive oil that was used in food and for lighting, and thanks to the export of foodstuffs and above all to the olive oil trade, the cities of this region attained a prosperous lifestyle. Today olive oil still holds an important place in the cookery of the Aegean region.

At the same time, local people have learned from the inhabitants of the Aegean islands how various wild plants and herbs can used in cooking. Nowadays, from mid-February when nature awakens from its winter sleep, it presents the cook with countless wild plants, and Aegean folk take full advantage of the possibilities. Moreover, the people of the Aegean have known since the dawn of history how to avail themselves in their cookery of the abundant crops of the sea. From generation to generation, until the present day, the people of this region have handed down their methods of cooking with exceptional skill, using the quality olive oil they produce and every kind of vegetable grown on their fertile soil.

Wild plants like dandelion, radish, mustard and garlic, which dwellers in the interior of the region ignore or of whose gastronomic properties they are unaware, are a great asset. Plants such as nettle, mallow, dock, garden glory, poppy, sheep's sorrel, fuzzy hair, and the wild asparagus known as *kedirgen* grow in great quantity. The locals know these plants and often gather them in the countryside.

If you go out into the countryside around Istanbul and see people collecting wild plants, you can wager that they hail from the Aegean. Most people from Istanbul don't recognize these plants; those who once knew them have forgotten them, so the probability is high that anyone you see gathering these plants, especially in springtime when they sprout fresh from the earth, is of Aegean origin.

Aubergines, of course, are not peculiar to the Aegean, but in no other region of our land will you come across so many different dishes using them. You will find varieties ranging from 'shouter' to 'slipper' and 'slipper roast'. Aegean artichokes are not the same as the *Bayrampaşa* artichokes of Istanbul – their globes are small, with abundant leaves. They are available at greengrocers for far longer than their *Bayrampaşa* kindred, and are used to make all sorts of dishes, from *dolmas* to pilafs.

Anyone who has ever eaten rubbery squid will be amazed at the fried squid of the Aegean, soft as Turkish delight. Also to be found are delicious squid salads, squid casseroles, squid *yahni* (stew with onions), and squid *dolma*. Also, one can never have enough of the taste of the local goat's and sheep's cheeses, among them *lor*, fresh goat's cheese, with its milky musk-like fragrance, and *çökelek*, made from skimmed milk, which is used in various dishes. When it is mixed with herbs and olive oil, it is called 'gypsy pilaf'. Unsalted *lor* cheese is made into delicious puddings.

Aegean cookery, though no such claim has ever been made for it, is a vegetarian's dream. In this respect, in comparison with the food of other lands, and indeed of other regions of Turkey, it is something special, with its countless vegetable and bean dishes and its raw or lightly cooked salads, its varied herbs and luscious olive oil.

Many of the dishes mentioned are common to all the lands surrounding the Mediterranean, but Turkey's Aegean region has a distinction that sets it apart and makes it *primus inter pares*, first among equals. In recent years the island of Crete, not far from the Aegean, has won worldwide fame for its Mediterranean cuisine. The Cretan diet has become a universal model, and the cuisine of the people of Turkey's Aegean shores is very similar to that of Crete. In traditional Cretan dishes, raw and cooked vegetables, beans, plentiful fresh and dried fruits, walnuts, olives and olive oil form the basis of the dishes, while red meat and animal fats have only a small part.

Aegean cuisine, which is so much in keeping with the contemporary understanding of nutrition, has developed over thousands of years. It is simple, yet exceptionally flavoursome. Nevertheless, while it is possible wherever one goes in other Mediterranean countries – Italy, France, Spain – to sample specialities with all the characteristics of the region, it is no easy task for a tourist in Turkey's Aegean cities or towns to find local dishes. The reason is that Turkish people mostly prepare and eat their delightful dishes in their own homes. When they feel like eating out, they prefer the specialities they cannot easily make for themselves. For example, they do not want to cook fish at home, because they do not want the house to smell of fish, so the whole family goes out 'to eat fish'. This is the main reason why there are so many fish restaurants along Anatolia's Aegean coast .

So what should we do if we want to taste the triumphs of Aegean cuisine? To my mind, the best Aegean food is to be found in the city of Ayvalik, where at every step one comes across restaurants abounding in excellent local dishes, each better than the last. (The next best choice is Izmir.) It's a good idea to ask the locals both here and in other towns for advice and to go to the restaurants they recommend. As for those who make the mistake of going to a restaurant in a big hotel in the hope of getting a decent regional meal, they will probably be disappointed.
Of course the best way of getting to know Aegean cuisine is to become a guest in a family home.

Market Food

by Sami Zubaida

Markets, historically, were the main locus of public food in Middle Eastern (and many other) cities. Cook-shops, located in the main bazaars, catered for market workers and traders. Typically, the poorer customers squatted outside or sat on stools eating, while the merchants and craft shop-owners would send their servants to fetch the food, to consume in their shops or private quarters. Customers in local cafés and *çayhanes* could also order food from neighbouring cook-shops, to consume with their beverages and *nargila* over a game of *tavla*. Many households would also send children or servants to collect items of prepared food for lunch. Most of these cook-shops specialized in particular items: the most common were (and remain) the *kebabçıs*, displaying various meats and grilling to order over charcoal burners (*mangal*). Others included *paçacıs*, specializing in broths of tripe, heads and feet (also, *iskembeci* in Turkish usage). Sweets and pastries continue to be common specialities: people sometimes ate *baklava* as a luxurious lunch. *Kubba/kebbe* (Arabic, Turkish: *içli köfte* as well as *çiğ köfte*) were other cook-shop specialities.

I write in the past tense uneasily, because many of these shops and stalls continue, and have indeed spread and multiplied. In more recent times, however, they have existed alongside and sometimes merged with restaurants, fast-food joints, cafés and bars, in various combinations. In the past they were the primary public outlet for cooked food, and the best enjoyed lofty reputations, with customers making special detours to sample their offerings.

In Istanbul, which has developed a rich and varied food and restaurant culture, some of the old market eateries have developed into top-class restaurants. They have, however, retained elements of the culture of their origins, and some of the characteristic repertoires of food. As such they are still known in some quarters as *esnaf lokantası*, *esnaf* being the term designating craft guilds, the main personnel of the old markets. Of course, the cook-shop staff themselves constituted separate guilds by speciality and craft.

Visits to Istanbul over the years, and a stay of a few months some years ago, have familiarized me with the different genres of restaurants in that city. I list here some of the favourite old restaurants and some of their offerings.

The repertoire of the *esnaf lokantası* consists of 'traditional' urban dishes of meat, chicken, vegetables and rice, almost never fish (to be found typically in the *meyhane*, tavern-turned restaurant, another genre of Istanbul eateries). Some will offer a few grills, notably a rotating skewer of *döner kebab*. They tend to cook in the morning for the lunch trade (their most active period); in the evening they have the same food, reheated. They don't serve alcohol, even when some of them, like Hacı Abdullah in Beyoğlu, have become tourist attractions. Hacı Baba, also in Beyoğlu, has been completely transformed into a tourist restaurant and does serve alcohol.

The menu includes soup: at least two every day. A typical pair is *mercimek* (lentils) and *paça*, theoretically head and hooves of lamb, but in fact now mostly a head soup. Other regular features are *sulu* stews of vegetables and meat: *tas* kebab, stewed meat, *etli* (with meat) vegetables, such as *bamya*, *patlıcan* or *kabak*, stuffed vegetables, notably *kabak* or *sarma* of leaves (*yaprak*), which could be vine leaves, fresh or salted, depending on the season, or various cabbage and chard leaves, such as *kara lahana*, or *pazı*. Pilafs feature regularly; plain white pilaf and often *iç pilavı*, 'stuffing' rice, enriched with chopped liver, onions and herbs. Some days a restaurant may have special dishes: *incik* (lamb knuckle or shank), stewed then covered with slices of fried aubergine and finished in the oven, served with parcels of the meat, on the bone, surrounded by aubergine slices, is a dish sometimes found in Hacı Abdullah. I once ate a delicious *fıstık pilavı*, dripping with butter and aromatic with pistachios, at the Levent branch of Konyalı. Kanaat, in Üsküdar, offered *Özbek pilavı*, rice cooked in meat juices and tomato, with chickpeas and lumps of meat on the bone.

Kanaat is one of the largest and most distinctive of this traditional type of restaurant. The entrance hall is lined with display counters offering a distinguished range of sweets and puddings, followed by another displaying cold foods. In one corner of the main dining area are the kitchens, displaying the daily variety of hot foods in trays and pots, which is the general style of these restaurants, though Kanaat has a distinctly wide variety. In one corner of the kitchen area is a vertical spit for *döner kebab*. A typical and peculiar sweet is *tavukogöğsü*, made of chicken breast with flour, sugar and milk, best as *kazandibi* when slightly burnt and caramelized. At Kanaat it is best combined with their plain creamy ice-cream, called *kaymaklı* (*kaymak* being thick, almost solid cream traditionally made from buffalo milk).

The 'globalization' of the city, its status as a world city with multinational enterprises and agencies, as well as tourism, adds to the richness and variety of its food culture. At the same time it weakens the old identities and distinctions. This trend is already eroding the distinctiveness of *esnaf lokantası*, many of them becoming tourist attractions for their folkloric and historic images. Others are adapting wider menus to cater for changing clientele.

Food, Music, Rossini and the Sultan

by Emre Aracı

'Music is food for the soul,' it is said, but when we talk about real food and musicians, one name stands out among a list of many distinguished composers and performers, and that is Gioacchino Rossini. No serious Rossini biography is without a section on the composer's gastronomical adventures. In fact, his love of food and indulgence in cooking and preparing dishes in the course of composing music is captured in some of the nicknames given to his arias, the most famous being 'Di Tanti Palpiti' from *Tancredi*, dubbed the 'rice *aria*' because, apparently, the maestro composed it while waiting for his *risotto* to cook. A similar story, reported by Alessandro Falassi, tells how 'once Rossini won a bet which entitled him to a turkey stuffed with truffles. The bet was not honoured, and in response to the continual requests of the maestro, the loser excused himself by claiming that the season was poor and quality truffles were just not to be found. 'Nonsense, nonsense,' blurted Rossini, 'those are just false rumours circulated by turkeys that don't want to be stuffed!' (*Rossini on Food, A Symphony of Tastes*, Culturekiosque Publications, 1996–2000).

As well as being a gourmet, Rossini also recognised other's musical tastes – in particular the Ottoman sultan Abdulmecid (1839–1861), for whom he composed a military march in 1854. The young sultan, an admirer of Rossini's operas thanks to the pioneering work of his master of music, Giuseppe Donizetti Pasha, was delighted by this new ceremonial march, so much so that Rossini was immediately decorated with the Order of Nichanı Iftihar. This colourful and lively march, which I had the pleasure of arranging for string orchestra and which we included in our first CD, European Music at the Ottoman Court, was often played by Ottoman regimental bands. Rather curiously, there is also a fine recording by the 'President's Own' US Marine Band.

Hearing Rossini's music on the streets of Constantinople in the nineteenth century was not unusual. It was also not unusual to find food and music taking their place side by side at court, as part of formal dinner procedures adopted from the European model. Military bands often played operatic music and marches during dinner, when elaborately decorated tables were laid out. Abdulmecid would never sit with his guests, although protocol had significantly changed by the time of Sultan Abdulhamid II. And when the Prince of Wales, the future King Edward VII, visited Constantinople in 1869 with Princess Alexandra, as the guest of Sultan Abdulaziz, they found themselves serenaded at the table by the Imperial military band:

> 'The band of eighty-four admirable musicians, all Turks taught by an Italian, play charmingly every evening at dinner,' wrote Sir William Howard Russell, who accompanied the royal party. He also recorded that 'the dinner at [the Palace of] Saleh Bazaar, served on gold and silver plate, was in all respects admirable. The Sultan's band under Guatelli Pasha, in the saloon outside, quite astonished the company by its excellent rendering of operatic music, the musicians, facing about, played 'God Save the Queen' (William Howard Russell, *A Diary in the East*, Routledge, 1869, Vol. II, pp.479–80.)

Elaborate bilingual menus in French and Ottoman printed for these kind of occasions were matched by the programme of music, presented in the same fashion and headed by the imperial cipher, the *tuğhra* of the sultan. An original copy which survives in my own personal archive goes back to the reign of Sultan Reşad. Dated Monday, 21 March 1910, the repertoire included Wagner's 'Tannhauser March' and the overture to *Rienzi*, Bizet's 'L'Arlésienne Suite', Mascagni's 'Cavalleria Rusticana' and Weber's 'Invitation à la Valse'. The second half, which probably followed the dinner, introduced a chamber version of the famous love duet from 'Tristan and Isolde' – a very appropriate choice for the court in Istanbul, since Sultan Abdulaziz was among the benefactors of the festival theatre at Bayreuth. The late sultan was also a composer of waltzes and polkas, his own works at times providing the musical backdrop at state dinners. Everyone was in for a surprise, therefore, when the band of the Grenadier Guards, under the baton of Dan Godfrey, started playing *La Gondole Barcarolle*', 'composed by His Imperial Majesty the Sultan' at a dinner given by the Prince of Wales at Marlborough House in London on the occasion of the state visit of the sultan to England in July 1867.

When I was asked to provide the music for the state dinner at Dolmabahçe Palace in Istanbul hosted by the Turkish president Ahmet Necdet Sezer in the summer of 2004 during the NATO summit, I immediately turned to my historical musical sources and scores for inspiration. The imposing ceremonial hall of Dolmabahçe, with its neo-baroque European–Ottoman style of architecture, its gigantic pillars and titanic four-tonne crystal chandelier, was the perfect setting to recreate the splendour of a bygone age of grand diplomacy. The strings of the Istanbul Chamber Orchestra were placed on the balcony, where traditionally orchestras in Ottoman times used also to be positioned. Sultan Abdulaziz's music again featured, alongside marches and dances by Giuseppe Donizetti, Sultan Murad V and Callisto Guatelli. Rossini's famous Abdulmecid March was also among my selections. This could well have been a nineteenth-century scene, apart from the three battleships guarding the palace and the helicopters scrambling above in heightened security, amid fears of a possible terrorist attack. The music, however, was well steeped in the seventeenth century, at least to begin with. I chose Lully's 'Marche pour la ceremonie des Turcs' for the entrance of the world leaders, a gesture highly appreciated by Jacques Chirac, who was later to express this in a personal letter written from the Elysée Palace. The food was prepared by Vedat Başaran, one of Turkey's leading cooks, who based it on original Ottoman palace menus and included the famous *lüfer balığı dolması* (bluefish filled with nuts and herbs). This was an evening of musical material constructed from original scores, and food prepared similarly from original recipes; a perfect union, and one which Rossini, I am sure, would have much appreciated.

Feasts and the Wedding Pilaf of Konya

by Nevin Halıcı

As for feasts, the Turks of Central Asia have kept alive their ancient customs and traditions. The first-known written source is Orhan Abideleri mentions that the ruler Bilge Kagan gave an evening banquet in honour of his late brother. In the eleventh century, during the feast (*eid*) and at the wedding of the Hans, banquets would be devised where folk would feast themselves from thirty-foot-high minarets of food. During the Selçuk period we find reference to dishes being served on golden trays. When we reach the Ottoman era we learn that banquets were given at which more than 100 varieties of dish were offered.

In present-day Anatolia we come across a variety of banquets to celebrate the different stages of life, such as circumcision or marriage, and one of the most important of these is the ancient 'Pilaf of Konya'. This feast is known also as pilaf or pilaf mound because pilaf is always served in great quantities. In addition to pilaf, it has become customary over the centuries to offer a range of other food. I researched this subject some twenty years ago when I interviewed eighty-year-old Havva Beton, who avowed that the pilaf of her maternal grandmother was unchanged to the present day. Only in the past twenty years have changes been admitted. Where once a whole shoulder or leg would be placed on top of the pilaf mound, nowadays cubes of fried lamb *kuş başı* (literally translated as 'size of a bird's head') are used instead. Another sign of the times is the substitution of Coca-Cola for puréed fruit at the end of the wedding feast.

In Konya it is traditional for the groom's family to provide the wedding meal. During the summer, meals are served *al fresco* on a number of tables, and in the winter every room in the house is converted into a dining space with tables (*sofra*) laid out for ten to thirteen people. The scale of the operation is impressive. The guest list can range from 1,000 to 10,000. Customarily the pilaf is served on Sunday morning at 8 am, so cooks will get together on Friday evening and work through Saturday to prepare the banquet. Two or three cooks over a period of two days are capable of dealing with even a large feast. The hosts will lend a hand in the cleaning of the rice and help with serving.

A week before the pilaf is made the host will get together with the cook to shop. Depending on the size of the banquet, 100 to 200 sheep, rice and other ingredients will be purchased and delivered to the cook by Friday afternoon. Cooking is done in huge cauldrons, usually in the garden or in a nearby field. The meat is cooked first. During my research in 1990, I observed master cook Mehmet Kar with two assistants over a twenty-four-hour period. On that occasion they cooked for 5,000 guests. It was during this time that I witnessed for myself the master/apprentice relationship, a relationship of love and respect that has been practised for centuries.

Cooking began on Friday evening when the two assistants arrived after finishing their day jobs. They inspected the ingredients, after having first greeted the master in the traditional way by kissing his hand. The next day they arrived very early and again greeted the master in the same way. The great cauldrons were set up, the meat washed and placed in the pots. The meat for the okra dish was then cut up. All this was done in silence, each of the three cooks watching for just a flicker of an eyebrow or the tiniest gesture of the head when communication was essential. Only very rarely, to avoid a potential calamity, would the master whisper 'not ready', words which would be instantly complied with. When he was pleased with the assistant, the master would affectionately pat him on the back, to the assistant's obvious delight.

By the afternoon the meat had boiled; this marked the halfway mark in the proceedings. This did not, however, mean that the cooks stood idle – it was now time to shell the pistachio nuts for the *helva*, sort the dessert raisins, trim the okra and carry out other tasks. While this was going on, the groom's parents would visit several times to make sure the cooks were happy and ask how things were progressing. Broth from the meat, with soaked bread, would be offered throughout the day to guests and, when they took a break, to the cooks as well.

In the afternoon the okra was cooked and the fruit-in-syrup prepared, as *zerde*, a saffron-flavoured sweet rice, was also made. After this, the cooks could take a break, to rest in the cool of the evening. Late at night the rice was soaked and, in the early hours of the morning, the cooking of the wedding pilaf began. Meats were fried and the semolina *helva* made. The pilaf and the *helva* would be kept warm over oak-wood embers. By the sunrise call to prayer all the dishes were ready. At the end of prayers the groom's father would bring the Hoca from the mosque to bless the food. During prayers the master cook would lift the lid of each pot just a little. After prayers the groom's father and all those present would be given food. After they had eaten each guest would leave a tip for the cooks in the trays where the food had been served.

At eight o'clock in the morning serving of the guests began – first the family and relatives, then the other guests. At this point I noticed a youngster having a quiet word with one of the assistant cooks, following which the youngster went over to the master cook and said something to him. The master nodded, as if to say 'agreed'. The youngster bowed and kissed the master's hand. It turned out that the assistant cook's wife was about to give birth in hospital, but such was the respect towards the master that the assistant had asked a friend to seek leave on his behalf.

The cooks, who had been working quietly for the past two days, were now most active – taking food to the tables and clearing up afterwards. More okra, meat and *helva* was requested by the next sitting. Non-meat dishes were served, immediately followed by half portions of the meat dish. Sometimes the meat dish would be requested to be 'submarine' or 'concealed', meaning that the meat would be placed on the dish and then covered with pilaf. You never see salt on the table at a Konya wedding banquet – everyone trusts the master cook's judgement to add just the right amount to each dish. Any food not consumed at the banquet would be given to the poor.

The final dish to be served after the *zerde* is fruit in syrup, known as a 'pausing dessert'. The sight of this dish is a signal for hungry guests to order more before proceedings come to an end.

The wedding pilaf of Konya and its preparation in open air is unique to our food culture. I would urge anyone visiting Konya to find an opportunity to sample it.

Embassy Menu and Recipes

from Mrs Handan Haktanır,
wife of H. E. the former Turkish Ambassador to London

Gala Dinner at the residence of H. E. the Turkish Ambassador and Mrs Handan Haktanır in aid of the Anglo-Turkish Society Scholarships Appeal

Menu

Aubergine in olive oil

Seafood pastry

Stuffed roast loin of lamb

Sautéed potatoes and mushrooms

Apricots filled with *crême fraiche* in an orange sauce

Wine: white and red

Coffee

Aubergine in olive oil

Imam Bayıldı

Serves 4–6

2 large aubergines
Olive oil
3–4 onions, chopped
3 tomatoes, chopped
3 cloves garlic, chopped
Paprika
Fresh parsley, chopped
Salt and freshly ground black pepper
Tomato purée

Preheat the oven to 180°C/350°F/gas mark 4. Wash the aubergines and cut crossways into three pieces. Heat a little olive oil in a deep frying pan and fry the aubergine on both sides until lightly browned. Fry the onions in a little more oil until soft, then add the tomatoes and garlic. Add paprika, parsley, salt and freshly ground black pepper and cook for around 5 minutes more. Put the aubergine slices on a baking tray and cover them with this filling. Mix the tomato purée with water, pour over the aubergines, and bake in the preheated oven for 20 minutes.

Seafood pastry

Deniz ürünlü börek

Serves 10–12

1 packet puff pastry
1kg/2lb 3oz mixed seafood
½ cup béchamel sauce
Fish seasoning
Oil
Egg yolk

For the béchamel

125ml hot milk
12g butter
12g plain flour
Pinch nutmeg
Salt
Freshly ground black pepper

Preheat the oven to 180°C/350°F/gas mark 4. For the sauce, melt butter in saucepan. Add flour, salt & pepper. Take off heat and gradually stir in milk, whisking well to ensure there are no lumps.

Roll out the pastry 0.5cm thick, then cut into squares and fill with the seafood mixture mixed with béchamel sauce. Fold the pastry from all four sides so that the mixture is covered. Place on an oiled baking tray, brush with egg yolk, and cook in the preheated oven for approximately 30 minutes.

Stuffed Roast Loin of Lamb with Sautéed Potato and Mushrooms

Sebzeli kuzu rosto sote patates ve mantar garnili

Serves 2–4

Loin of lamb (boneless if available)
Bunch spring onions
4-5 mushrooms
1 large onion
Olive oil

For the marinade

Salt
Freshly ground black pepper
Paprika
Olive oil

Bone the lamb if necessary and make sure the meat is quite flat by kneading it down with a rolling pin or board. Mix the salt, pepper, paprika and oil in a dish, and add the lamb and leave to marinate overnight. Next day, preheat the oven to 200°C/350°F/gas mark 0. Cut the vegetables into small cubes and fry in a little oil for 2–3 minutes. Remove the lamb from the marinade and spread with the vegetables. Shape the stuffed meat into a roll, making sure all the edges are sealed.

Put the lamb on a baking tray, wrap in foil, and cook in the preheated oven for 1 hour. Serve with rice, sautéed potatoes and mushrooms.

Apricots Filled with Fresh Cream

Kremalı kayisi, portakal soslu

Serves 8–10

455g/1lb/3 cups dried apricots, soaked in water overnight
455g/1lb/2½ cups sugar
225ml/8fl oz/1 cup double cream
Rind of 1 orange

Drain the soaked apricots and lay out on a tray or dish, reserving the water. Set aside a cup of sugar and put the rest into a pan. Add the reserved soaking water and boil for 10 minutes. Leave to cool. Whip the cream and fill the apricots with it.

Cut the orange rind into long strips and put into a small pan with water to cover. Boil for 2 minutes, then remove the rind from the pan. Put the reserved glass of sugar, a little water and a few drops of lemon juice into another pan and cook until caramelized. Stir the orange rind into the caramel, sprinkle over the apricots and serve.

A few more recipes from the Embassy

Courgette Meze

Kabaklı meze

Serves 6–8

3 courgettes
Salt
3 tablespoons yoghurt
2 tablespoons mayonnaise
1 clove garlic, crushed
Fresh dill leaves

Cut the courgettes into chunks and cook gently in salted boiling water until tender. Drain well and leave to cool. Mix together the yoghurt, mayonnaise and garlic, stir in the courgettes, and season with salt. Sprinkle with dill leaves before serving.

Honey Crisp Doughnuts

Lokma

Serves 8–10

For the batter

2 eggs
2 tablespoons yoghurt
5 heaped tablespoons plain flour
2 teaspoons baking powder
Pinch of salt
Oil for frying

For the syrup

1 slice lemon
225ml/8fl oz/1 cup water
400g/14oz/2 cups sugar

To make the syrup, put the water into a small pan, add the sugar, and bring to the boil and simmer for half an hour, until the sugar has dissolved. Leave to cool.

Put the batter ingredients into a mixing bowl and stir to combine. It should have the consistency of a cake mixture (add more flour if necessary). Heat the oil in a large frying pan. Drop 6–7 small pieces of batter into the hot oil and increase the heat, turning a few times, until they take on a nice brownish colour. Then reduce the heat and add a second lot, and so on.

When the *lokma* are done, remove from the oil and dip immediately into the cool syrup, removing after a few minutes.

Walnut Pâté

Cevizli pate

Serves 4–6

115g/4oz/1 cup walnuts, broken into small pieces
Juice of ½ lemon
2 cloves garlic
2 tablespoons olive oil
Pinch of ground cumin
Toasted bread
Fresh parsley leaves

Put all the ingredients except the parsley into a blender and pulse for a few seconds. Spread on small pieces of toasted bread.

Serve garnished with parsley.

Celeriac and potato purée

Patatesli kereviz püresi

Serves 8–10

30g/1oz margarine
2 onions, chopped
455g/1lb celeriac, peeled and cubed
455g/1lb potatoes, peeled and cubed
225ml/8fl oz/1 cup chicken stock
Salt and freshly ground black pepper
55g/2oz butter
Fresh parsley leaves

Melt the margarine in a frying pan, add the onions and cook until softened. Add the celeriac and potatoes and continue cooking until tender. Add the stock and cook for a further 20 minutes. Season well with salt and freshly ground black pepper. Mash the vegetables with a fork, adding the butter while still hot.

Serve as a side dish with chicken or meat, garnished with parsley.

Afterword

By Belma Ötüş-Baskett

My American husband, having received a Fulbright grant to teach American literature at Hacettepe University in Ankara, began to read in depth about the country where he was to spend the next year, and as an adventurous food-lover, he was intrigued at this new gustatory vista, for he had never eaten Turkish food. Three decades ago the possibility of doing so did not really come to mind for a Midwesterner, even on trips to Chicago, New York or San Francisco. Certainly it did not come to the mind of his department chairman, who, at the farewell party, banteringly advised him: 'Don't get lost in the Anatolian wilds. Imagine being condemned to eating Turkish food for the rest of your life!' This jest, in fact, anticipated my husband's fate – happily so, he assures me, for being married to me he is doing just that. 'I knew what I was doing when I married a Turkish cook,' he is given to remark.

As Raphaela Lewis says in her introduction to this book, for centuries up until the demise of the Ottoman Empire what was meant by 'Turkish cuisine' was the cooking at the Imperial Palace and a few wealthy houses in Istanbul. The lands of the empire were vast, however, and there must have been great variation in the cooking from region to region. Some of the chefs would have come from other parts of the empire, or have been aware of dishes from those parts: for example, the impact of the Circassians and the Albanians can be seen in dishes such as Circassian chicken (*çerkes tavuğu*) and Albanian liver (*arnavut ciğeri*). But if there were dishes from other regions, they must have been adapted and refined for presentation in accordance with the Istanbul palate. The most highly regarded cooks in Istanbul were from Bolu and Gerede, and they may have brought with them some regional accents, although they came to Istanbul at a very young age and were trained in the kitchens by older cooks expert in the Istanbul taste.

The everyday food eaten by the general populace was different: simpler, less refined. 'Good food' was available for them on *bayrams*, feast days and for *iftar*, the breaking of the fast after dark during Ramadan, and also on special days of royal celebration such as weddings, accessions to the throne, circumcision parties of princes, when the sultan offered it to them in public squares. On feast days and breaking the fast nights, the rich would provide healthy meals for the poor, consisting of soup, meat, rice and dessert. Leftover food from both the palace and the homes of the rich was always given to the poor, discreetly on the same day from the back door. Food was never wasted and no one went hungry.

Although smaller than the Ottoman Empire, Turkey remains a vast country, extending to 780,000 square kilometres. Surrounded by three seas, it includes many plains, high mountains and extensive plateaus. As the geography and climate vary, so does the produce, resulting in different regional cuisines such as those of the Black Sea, the Mediterranean, the mountain areas, the plateaus in the hinterland and so on. For example, Black Sea cooking offers a wide range of fish dishes, especially *hamsi* (anchovy): you can have *hamsi tavası* (fried), *buğulama hamsi* (steamed), *hamsili pilav* (with rice), and also *hamsi turşusu* (pickled). Similar varieties exist for other local fish such as *kalkan* or plaice. Again special to this area is the corn bread and the big rustic loaves of *vakfı-kebir*. Fish in the Izmir area includes sea bream (*çupra*) and *trança*, for which it is difficult to find an English word. Olive oil is used more extensively in cooking, including for fried eggs and omelettes.

The important Mediterranean fish is *lagos*, again with no real English equivalent. Purslane – *semizotu* – grows abundantly in the area and is used in the local *börek* as a filling. There are many, many more regional varieties.

Returning to Istanbul cooking, it can be said that it is to a considerable extent a continuation of the palace tradition. However, the cuisine there – and that of Izmir and Ankara as well – has in recent decades increasingly become mingled with others as a result of the many foreign influences through embassies, consulates, businesspeople and tourists. Previously Turks had mostly relied on their own cuisine, but non-Turkish restaurants are now available throughout those cities. The popularity of Italian cooking has begun in Turkey, with a few Italian restaurants opening. This fad follows that of Chinese restaurants somewhat earlier, although there are only a few of these establishments, possibly because of the difficulty of getting authentic ingredients.

Turks have become very successful in exporting their cuisine. This process began in the nineteenth century, when the Balkan lands broke away from the empire. There were many emigrants, both Turkish and non-Turkish, especially to the United States and Canada. They took their cooking traditions with them, and many dishes with Turkish names. Such names began to appear on the menus of many restaurants worldwide, Turkish or otherwise. Among those most frequently found in non-Turkish restaurants are the following: *dolma*, *lokma*, and *imam bayıldı*.

Some emigrants took up farming when they reached their destinations, growing the vegetables they knew from their homeland. If it was dairy farming, they were sure to make yoghurt. When they opened restaurants, their principal ethnic dishes were on offer. At first, most popular abroad were kebabs. I often think of kebabs as the Turkish version of 'fast foods', with the meat grilled rather than fried, however, and always accompanied by vegetables, onions, parsley and tomatoes. A significant modification abroad has been the substitution of beef for lamb, and a toning down of spices to accommodate foreign palates. Otherwise, in the nineteenth century, Turkish cooking in Turkey and abroad remained traditional, in accordance with the respective regions.

In the twentieth century, owing to great upheavals in Turkey and elsewhere, changes began to come about. Following the Russian Revolution many White Russians emigrated to Turkey, especially Istanbul. Often they were from aristocratic backgrounds and accustomed to the pleasures of fine dining, and some opened restaurants and cafés offering good food and accompanied by entertainment. Previously, Turks had eaten at restaurants only when necessary, but with the influx of the Russians habits began to change, as a very cosmopolitan restaurant scene developed. Dishes such as *borç*, chicken Kievski, *böf strogonof* were introduced, and within a few decades had become part of the menus of many Turkish restaurants as well as those of the two Russian restaurants of the era – which are still operating in Beyoğlu today, the old Rus (Russian) and the Rejans.

Another factor to be considered with regard to the development and extension of Turkish cuisine is the effect of the Second World War, when great numbers of troops from Europe and North America were posted to distant places. American troops, when they returned home, had generally developed a taste for different, often spicier foods than before. In England close relations with India had helped develop a taste for kebabs and the spicy foods encountered there over a long period. Generally speaking, once people expand their tastes, it becomes easier for them to accept and even crave other cuisines.

There were various reasons for the Turkish contribution to this globalization. There were great developments in transportation, with faster trains and ships, air travel, international coach links, better highways and widespread private ownership of automobiles. Moreover, as the rebuilding of Europe after the war created great demand for workers, individuals and families from Turkey and the Balkans flooded into a number of countries. Again, they opened small groceries and restaurants to accommodate the tastes of their ethnic communities, but soon friends and co-workers were introduced to Turkish food. I recall that during the 1983 coup in Turkey, when I was flying to a conference in Germany, customs officials thoroughly searched the suitcases of all the passengers. Those of guest workers displayed great quantities of the food they were taking with them: bulgur, *tarhana*, tomato and pepper paste, even huge watermelons. As the years passed and the numbers increased, enterprising Turks in Germany started to import many foods from Turkey. During holidays returning Turks sometimes brought friends and neighbours home with them, further introducing many to Turkish food. Also, as tourism in Turkey expanded, more foreigners began to sample the food on offer. Returning to Germany, but in other countries as well, the travellers provided a market for the kind of things they had enjoyed on vacation, and regular supermarkets began to stock 'exotic' foods, a practice in the accelerating globalization of foods, applicable to other ethnic groups as well.

I remember going to Germany in the 1970s with my then teenage son. He would not be content until I took him to a Turkish neighbourhood for him to eat, as I recall, a kebab, *kuru fasulye* (dried bean stew) and *beyaz peynir* (white cheese). His taste was perhaps analogous to that of some Americans who, when they travel, often want their McDonald's hamburger or Kentucky Fried Chicken. In the late 1980s I travelled with American college students around the world, teaching on a university ship. At every port the vast majority of the students rushed ashore to find American fast food. Demonstrating the intricacies of globalization, in addition to the American favourites noted above, the students often wanted deep-pan pizza.

As the originally Italian pizza went global – or, at least, became Americanized – so did the Turkish kebab. Originally kebab shops attracted Turks from Anatolia or Cyprus who had ventured abroad seeking better economic opportunities but now kebabs are available everywhere, often with Turkish bread or pitta bread. Kebabs have become largely generic, with a nod to regional differences, probably according to the taste and knowledge of the kebab maker, or in an attempt to attract a loyal clientele for a particular shop.

After the first and second generation of shops, the new generation offers more upmarket, and even first-rate, restaurants in the centres of major cities around the world – London, New York, San Francisco, Vienna, Sydney, etc. In all these cities it is possible to buy most of the Turkish ingredients in speciality shops, but also, more recently, in supermarkets.

In the last half of the twentieth century there was a great demographic shift within Turkey as millions moved from rural areas to the large cities, especially Istanbul, Ankara and Izmir where they would have access to jobs, schools, hospitals and, hopefully, a better life. Many missed the food they had been used to and, consequently, regional restaurants opened in the metropolitan centres. Bursa was well known for the best lamb in Turkey, and Bursa kebab first appeared in Istanbul and then later in Ankara. It was followed by Adana kebab, and now almost all kebab restaurants offer a long list of regional kebab dishes. *Kebabçıs* from Gaziantep and, for example, Urfa, introduced pomegranate juice (*nar suyu*) for salad flavouring. Thus the more remote areas became represented on the culinary scene of the big cities. In this widening of the availability of regional dishes two trends were evident. At first the differences tended to be blurred – standardized to fit in with the more traditional cuisine expected in urban centres. A later trend, however, capitalized on these differences, emphasizing their distinctively regional offerings. Now a place or area name may denote the kind of food available, but it can be found in a wide range of restaurants. However, there are some foods that have remained regional and local, showing no likelihood of being accepted internationally. They are mostly offal, such dishes as *işkembe çorbası* (tripe soup), *paça* (lamb knuckles) and *kelle* (roasted head of lamb). If these were ever found abroad it would only be in Turkish neighbourhoods, and they are rarely seen now even in Turkey. On coach journeys, at various stops one used to be able to obtain the local dishes, but nowadays coaches stop only in designated places, where restaurants and gift shops offer standardized 'tourist' fare.

Recent discoveries in medicine and dietetics have been a boon to the spread of Turkish cooking. When I was in the US for an extended period, beginning in the late 70s, the fad of healthy eating was often the topic of conversation. My friends and acquaintances started modifying, or at least talking about modifying, their diets in the direction of healthy eating. Columns in newspapers, magazine articles, even books came out in increasing numbers advising everyone to add dried vegetables, fresh vegetables and fruit to their diet in place of less healthy food. The desirability of eating more fibre was emphasized, and yoghurt became almost a staple in the Western diet. Olive oil became recognized as the healthiest oil. It turned out, to my great satisfaction, that what was meant by the 'healthy diet' was actually the food I had grown up on in Turkey. Some people appeared annoyed that I knew so much about what was entirely new to them with regard to diet. Most, however, bombarded me with questions and requests for recipes, the most frequent request being for instructions about dried bean and lentil dishes as proteins to replace meat.

In keeping with this trend, as people considered the vegetables on offer more carefully, more varieties appeared in markets. Okra and aubergine were the two vegetables Westerners rarely cooked, but this began to change. And they have begun to adapt the cooking of more familiar vegetables in the direction of Turkish practice, with the use of olive oil, onions, garlic and tomatoes, learning and enjoying different ways of cooking. Bulgur (cracked wheat), for example, the poor Turkish peasant's daily gruel, came to grace the most refined tables. All of these items that had been available only in a few speciality shops began to appear on supermarket shelves. In a few years, what may be considered a gastronomic revolution was taking place around me in Michigan, where I was teaching at the time. Later, moving to London, I found that my friends here, being closer to the Middle East and the Mediterranean, were more familiar with Turkish foods, but here, too, the change in diet taking place at that time was clearly evident, even in meals served in public institutions.

The importance of salads in the Turkish cuisine is well-known. It could be said that salads are important in most cuisines. Before the 70s or 80s, however, it seemed to me that groceries offered very little variety in salad leaves – and they were expensive. Now, supermarkets abound in an ever more confusing range of choices, many combinations even washed and ready to serve. It is thus easy to have a salad with every meal, or even a salad to constitute a meal. This is not owing to the Turkish cuisine, but it is certainly in keeping with it.

Turkish desserts vary from the very elaborate, and heavy, *baklava* to milk puddings (e.g. *sütlaç, tavuk göğsü*) to fruit-based lighter sweets, bread pudding with sour cherries, quince and apricot desserts (*vişneli ekmek, ayva and kayısı tatlısı*). In the summer most dessert shops are closed, however, and heavy desserts are not served in either restaurants or homes. Then 'coolers' (*soğukluk*) are served for dessert – melon or watermelon, nicely chilled. Even in winter it is not customary to eat dessert after every meal; fruit is often substituted, a practice in accordance with contemporary dietary recommendations.

At the beginning of the twentieth century, Turkish food was popular – and readily available – in many countries, even though it may be called by more general names such as 'healthy diet', 'health food', 'Mediterranean food' or 'Middle Eastern food' – or by the names of the several nations in the Balkan Peninsula. Such names usually denote 'Turkish food', owing to the fact that these countries were part of the vast Ottoman Empire which ruled that part of the world for many centuries. With the demand in the palace for good food and new tastes, Ottoman cooking had been continually revised, augmented and refined.

Since the mid-twentieth century, Turks have increasingly come into contact with other cuisines, resulting in still further changes. A second generation of restaurateurs is now on the scene, and their ambitions and training have led them to open excellent restaurants. A tendency of twenty-first century restaurants seems to be the blurring of their ethnic origins. Lately Turks have opened restaurants, bars and cafés with names not indicative of Turkey. In such establishments, traditional Turkish dishes are often served as well as dishes of other ethnic origins. Also, creative Turkish restaurateurs/cooks/chefs are experimenting with certain traditional dishes and even inventing others, dependent on the ingredients available in locations around the world.

In Vienna, London, New York and Sydney, I have noted at least one Turkish restaurant listed among the top ten or twenty. Interestingly, in Tashkent, the Jules Verne tourism agency takes their clientele, bored with the monotonous Uzbekestan 'in-tourist' fare, to a Turkish restaurant run by two Turkish brothers. As there has not been mass emigration from Turkey to the east, individual initiative is responsible for any appearance of Turkish cuisine in this part of the world.

The second and third generation of 'modern' Turkish restaurateurs have experimented with new dishes – a kind of Turkish 'nouvelle cuisine' – as well as with non-traditional decor. Largely disappeared are the old 'Turkish-style' restaurants, with typical Turkish carpets. Copper and Kütahya plates on the walls have been replaced by subtler suggestions of Turkey, some with minimalist international decor or other imaginative alternatives. In New York and London, one may find in open-plan restaurants that chefs wear classic white caps – or perhaps red, reminiscent of the Ottoman *fez*, while cooking in state-of-the-art kitchens. In Sydney, the best ten restaurants of the city have formed a consortium with an upmarket catering service. They are online with extensive menus – and two of the group are Turkish. All of this is in addition to the restaurants in the Turkish neighbourhood and the fast-food kebab places near all the 'tourist' sites such as beaches and parks.

All Turkish restaurants in Australia have an earthen oven (*fırın*), gyro (*döner*) and open-kitchen arrangement. The Turkish staff speak very good English. They are all family establishments, with family members sharing responsibilities, the younger generation having been educated in Australia. One curious restaurant advertises itself as offering 'Mexican/Turkish Cuisine', serving dried beans with mince (*kıymalı kuru fasulye*) and black beans (*barbunya*). Their aim, as stated, is to capture the exigencies of the Australian palate. Of the Turkish restaurants in central Sydney, Samsun and Erciyes are notable. The premier Turkish restaurant in Canberra serves 'Ottoman Modern Turkish Cuisine', catering to the diplomatic community in the capital.

On a leafy street in central Warsaw is the Istanbul restaurant, serving full-fledged Turkish cuisine in expensive surroundings. Next door is the Istanbul bar, café and kebab place – all this in a beautiful area built before the Second World War. The presence of excellent Turkish restaurants around the world is further evident in such eateries as the long-established Kervansaray, on the Opern Ring in Vienna, and Divan, in Washington DC. In New York, Turkish restaurants of all sizes and shapes abound, so I shall only mention Üsküdar on 2nd Avenue and Derviş, the best of them all, located in central Manhattan on 47th Street between 6th and 7th Avenues. It has a tasteful bar section in addition to the spacious restaurant decorated in the latest minimalist style.

Turkish restaurants in the US are still confined to the few big cosmopolitan centres, with, for example, Ali Baba (with music and belly dancing) and Üsküdar (not a chain) in San Francisco. In other parts of the US Turkish dishes like *imam bayıldı*, *köfte*, etc, appear on the menus of Greek and Middle Eastern restaurants.

Turning to Britain, one can see that Turkish restaurants are everywhere. To single out a few, one may mention the Bosphorus, situated on the newly redesigned quay in Cardiff Bay, where one can replicate a Turkish experience by eating fresh fish on the waterfront, reminiscent of the Iskele restaurants found in every village along the Bosphorus. There is also a good Turkish restaurant in Bath, situated on the Crescent.

That Turkish restaurants of every type are now part of the London scene has been appreciatively noted by the *Time Out Eating and Drinking Guide*. Some twenty restaurants are listed, many red-starred as being 'very good indeed', and many more green-starred for good value. The uninitiated diners are aided by a menu glossary of nearly 100 terms to introduce them to 'one of the world's great cuisines'.

Kebab vans are to be found in every section of London and Istanbul *İşkembecisi* – tripe shops – operate in the Turkish area of north London. Of the major restaurants, two of the longest-established are the Efes: one a regular dining-room and the other with a Turkish floor-show complete with belly dancer. One of the new restaurateurs is a Turk in Richmond whose eatery, Escale, claimed to serve Mediterranean food, though a big marquee now proclaims 'Authentic Turkish Cuisine', perhaps an instance of the vagaries of international politics. Indeed, Escale does offer typical Turkish fare: the *meze* plate as starters and kebabs as main dishes.

Tas restaurant opened with a traditional Turkish menu on The Cut near Waterloo, with another opening soon after on Borough High Street with live music on some evenings. Offering lighter fare, two Tas Pide restaurants followed, one near the Globe Theatre and the other on Farringdon Road. Recently another Tas restaurant opened near the British Museum and a very attractive complex, Ev, has been added, under the arches of Waterloo East station. It comprises a restaurant with an adjoining bar on one side and a delicatessen and organic grocery on the other. The furnishings, all imported from Turkey, provide a décor of minimalist luxury, with a few well-chosen pieces including contemporary floor tiling and glittering chandeliers hanging from the high-arched ceiling of the dining area facing the open kitchen. The bar area, seemingly favoured by a younger crowd, has a lighter menu. The delicatessen and organic grocery is a delight to browse in, with enticing Turkish food and artefacts appetizingly and attractively displayed, accompanied by the delicious aroma of their own bakery. The Ev menu specializes in authentic Turkish offerings, including many kinds of fish as well as meat and chicken. Particularly notable in this new venue is its spaciousness, which has allowed the creation of an artistic space indoors, and a big, pleasant area outdoors, all augmented by contemporary live music.

Hüseyin Özer, of Sofra fame, seems to have his finger on the pulse of London trends in Turkish restaurants. He first launched the Sofra in Shepherd Market, which proliferated into a number of Sofras in central London, followed by Sofra cafés, with open-air seating in many areas. Now the cafés are gone but there are five restaurants and counting – in

Mayfair, Covent Garden, St Christopher's Place, St John's Wood and Exmouth Market – with a sixth soon to open in Tower Place. (Also, a Sofra London has opened in Taksim Square in Istanbul.) Özer, near Oxford Circus, is their upmarket eatery, with minimalist but subtle Turkish motifs. Thus the Turkish restaurant abroad has taken its cosmopolitan/international expertise back to home territory.

This book was conceived as a labour of love to ensure scholarships to orphans in Turkey. Some sections are meant as food for thought and other sections with recipes and suggestions approach the style of more conventional cookbooks. We hope you enjoy it.

Contributors

Feride Alp is Director of the Turkish-British Chamber of Commerce and Industry.

Emre Aracı is one of Turkey's leading younger generation of musicologists.

Richard Cawley is a TV chef and writer.

Gönül Çilasun is a designer of leisurewear, winner of international awards and writer of vegetarian cookbooks.

Sally Clarke is an award-winning chef and owner of Clarke's restaurant, bakery and shop in Kensington, London.

Victoria Combe is a magazine journalist.

Roz Denny has written over 30 cookbooks, often with other well-known chefs, and she is a food media consultant.

Josceline Dimbleby has written seven cookbooks and is a lecturer on food.

Sevim Gokyıldız is President of the Turkish Chapter of the Mediterranean Food Council.

Nadir Güllü (Güllüoğlu is used with the Baklava title) is Chairman of the Turkish Gourmets Association.

Nevin Halıcı is one of Turkey's foremost writers. Her most recent publication is *Sufi Cuisine* (Saqi).

Eric Hansen is a worldwide travel writer based in San Francisco.

Ainsley Harriott's TV cooking series is now seen in 24 countries. His aim is to 'make cooking easy and fun'.

Abdullah Korun runs Hacı Abdullah, off Istiklal, serving traditional Ottoman cuisine. Many writers and travellers make the restaurant one of their first stops to eat delicious authentic Turkish food when visiting Istanbul.

Mehmet Kurakahveciler is known as Turkey's 'Coffee King'. Devotees included J.S. Bach, who composed the *Coffee Cantata*, and writers Molière, Pierre Loti and Victor Hugo.

Turgut Kut is a culinary historian and writer.

Nico Ladenis is a food writer and restaurant owner.

Nigella Lawson is a 'Food Goddess', food writer and TV chef, who has her own range of cookware.

Raphaela Lewis lectured on Turkish sociology and cuisine, and is the author of *Everyday Life in Ottoman Turkey*.

Canan Maxton is an interpreter, party hostess and organiser.

Anton Mosimann is a top chef who has written many books. His Mosimann Industries includes Mosimann Academy, Mosimann Party Service and an expanding range of Mosimann merchandising.

Ahmet Örs is a journalist, editor and food writer.

Belma Ötüş-Baskett is a writer, translator and lecturer at universities here, in the USA and in Turkey.

Hüseyin Özer is the owner of Sofra and Özer restaurants in London and in Turkey, and author of the *Sofra* cookbook.

Ali Pasiner was a writer and President of the Amateur Fishermen's Association.

Gary Rhodes is a TV chef, author and restaurant owner.

Claudia Roden is an award-winning writer and broadcaster, known as the 'chef's chef', particularly for her Mediterranean cooking. The latest of her 23 books is *Arabesque*, covering Morocco, Turkey and Lebanon.

Tuğrul Şavkay was a food writer and founder of many food and beverage associations.

Osman Serim is a food writer and restaurant development consultant.

Semih Sömer is President of the Turkish Kitchen Club.

Berrin Torolsan is a food writer and Publishing Director of the prestigious magazine *Cornucopia*.

Lesley Waters is a popular TV chef and runs her own cookery school in Dorset.

Jane Whiter is a chef at on the food advisory board of Westminster Classic Tours, one of the UK's leading tour operators for Turkey and the Greek Islands.

Antony Worrall Thompson is a prolific, award-winning TV chef and restaurant owner, and has own range of kitchen linens.

Vefa Zat is founder and honorary life member of the Barmen's Association.

Sami Zubaida is Emeritus Professor of Politics and Science at Birkbeck College, University of London, and also writes about food.

Photo Credits

Composition *Turkish Culture and Tourism Office*
Galatas Bridge restaurants *Sally Mustoe*
Istanbul stall *Rebecca Erol*
Cookbook pages *Turgut Kut*
Stuffed vine leaves *Anton Mosimann*
Falafel Rebecca Erol
Chilled yogurt and cucumber dip *K. Mewes/Cephas*
Turkish aubergine *Heino Banderob/Cephas*
Spinach soup *Canan Maxton*
Yoghurt bowl *K. Mewes/Cephas*
Aubergines *Rebecca Erol*
Imam bayildi Clive Streeter/Getty Images
Cauliflower *Gönül Cilasun*
Pepper salad *Gönül Cilasun*
Artichokes *Gönül Cilasun*
Celeriac with mushrooms *Gönül Cilasun*
Fish *courtesy of the Turkish Culture and Tourism Office*
Stuffed mussels *Michael Brauner/Cephas*
Seabass *Michael Brauner/Cephas*
Red mullet *Rebecca Erol*
Macaroni and meat pie *Uwe Bender/Cephas*
French beans *Gönül Cilasun*
Simit seller Naim Kula
Börek Anton Mosimann
Lamb *Luzia Ellert/Cephas*
Lahmacun Canan Maxton
Turkish delight *Naim Kula*
Kadayıf Rebecca Erol
Compote of apricots, prunes and oranges *Rebecca Erol*
Apricots with cream, almond and pistachio *Rebecca Erol*
Baklava Turkish Culture and Tourism Office
Hacı Abdullah Naim Kula
Helva Naim Kula

Orchid *Barbara and Zafer Baran*
Flaming pears *Handan Haktanır*
Sherbet *Achim Deimling-Ostrinsky/Cephas*
Yoghurt drink *Canan Maxton*
Rakı Damir Begovic/Cephas
Fountains *Naim Kula*
Turkish coffee *Naim Kula and Sally Mustoe*
Cheese *Rebecca Erol*
Spices *Ibrahim Ay*
Olives *Martin Skultety/Cephas*
Aegean boat spread *Westminster Classic Tours*
Döner kebab Thomas Wober/Cephas
Rossini *Emre Aracı*
Wedding feast, Konya *Nevin Halıcı*
Istanbul *Rebecca Erol*

Index